No-Sew Knitting

No-Sew Knitting

21 stylish designs
for seam-free knits

CHRISTINE BOGGIS

Contents

Get around

Get relaxed

Get involved

No sew, no stress

Seamless designs can help you knit your way to crafty relaxation and take all the uncertainty out of the finished project.

Why do you knit? I started knitting because I wanted to make things I couldn't find in the shops, but now I do it to relax. In times of stress, anxiety, depression or social unease, the soothing movements of yarn and needles can calm me; the sense of purpose knitting gives me relieves feelings of being out of place, and it's simply a lovely thing to do.

I want everyone to be able to feel the relaxing benefits of knitting, and for me one of the best ways to make knitting more relaxing is to make it seam-free. When I started out making designs from traditional knitting patterns in pieces, I was often disappointed by the results of my own sewing. That is definitely down to my own lack of expertise in that area, but it created an element of stress: all the time I was knitting, I had a sense that these hours and precious materials might be wasted in a finished object that wasn't quite right.

Knitting garments in one piece, whether that be from the top down, the bottom up, the centre out or side to side, is my way of banishing that particular stressor and making my knitting a more enjoyable experience. Single-piece designs allow you to see your finished object emerging from your needles as you go. When I'm knitting a top-down jumper I can try it on as I work, making sure that every part of it fits, right down to the sleeves – I can keep knitting until they actually cover my extra-long Mr Tickle arms!

CRAFTING DESIGNS

My designs are all about the joy of knitting. I often get inspiration from garments I see other people wearing. When this happens, my first thought is: how can I recreate that by hand? My second is: how can I make it fun? Many of my designs combine interesting lace and cable panels with simple stocking stitch sections – the aim is to offset the technical

challenge of knitting a more or less intricate pattern with the relaxing element of simple rhythmic stitches you can do in front of the TV or on a commuter train.

It also aims to make adjusting fit as simple as possible. For example, in *Magdalene* all the tricky stuff is done first, in the panels; afterwards you simply knit out sideways until the body is the right size for you, before working the sleeves in the round. All of the top-down jumpers can be tried on as you work and adjusted to suit, while for the bottom-up knits you may need a measuring tape and a bit of maths.

HOW TO KNIT AND RELAX

There are three main ways knitting can alleviate stress and anxiety, help you relax and even lift your mood. The first is the simple, tactile act of knitting itself. Scientific research has found there are benefits to our bodies and minds from the way the needles cross the body in knitting. Feeling soft fibres passing through our hands can be very soothing, and making stitches one by one can be used as a tool to calm breathing and slow the heart rate in times of difficulty.

On the other side of the coin, the creative outlet of knitting and its technical challenges can be so absorbing that they distract us from other worries and intrusive thoughts, giving us a valuable break from our own busy brains, even if only for a short time. This kind of intense mental exercise is really good for knitters of all ages.

And then there's the finished product. If you spend your days in the kind of mindless, repetitive tasks that are never finished – like housework, childcare and, in some cases, paid work – it can be so satisfying to actually produce something you can complete, see, touch and enjoy. That alone is enough to lift the spirits.

ALTERNATIVE CONSTRUCTION

This book aims to introduce you to different ways of working patterns – hats, jumpers, cardigans and socks are knitted from the top down, from the bottom up, side to side and from the centre out. Maybe you'll find a favourite direction and stick with that – or maybe you'll try everything and still want more. You can get even more ideas from the designers who have inspired me – meet some of them on page 10.

The volume is divided into three sections: *Get around* is an introduction to seam-free knitting, featuring simple hats, cowls, mittens and other accessories to get you started on the techniques you will use throughout the book and beyond. *Get relaxed* focuses on stress-free, in-the-round knitting and the kind of sweaters and accessories that allow you to knit on and on without worry of any kind, getting into the soothing rhythm of your needles and yarn. *Get involved* is the home of more complex designs with some unusual techniques which I hope you'll enjoy as much as I have!

GETTING AROUND TENSION

Nearly every knitting designer will encourage you to knit a swatch before you cast on your project, and I am no different. In each of these patterns you will find a tension guide – the number of stitches and rows you should get over 4in (10cm) square.

While they are not always 100% reliable, swatches should tell you if your tension matches the tension in the project. If you knit the swatch and it comes out bigger than expected, that means your tension is too loose and you should try going down a needle size or two. If it is smaller, your tension is too tight and you should try a bigger needle. It is far better to find this out after knitting a small swatch than after casting off a whole cardigan!

Many knitters find their tension is slightly different when they are knitting in the round from when they are knitting back and forth, so your tension swatch should match the way you are knitting in the pattern. For in-the-round designs, I love knitting swatch mitts.

SWATCH MITTS

1. Start by measuring your wrist and the circumference of your palm. Mine are both roughly 7in (18cm), so I like to cast on around 8in (20cm) worth of stitches. This makes the maths very easy as I only need to double the stitch count for 4in (10cm) on the yarn band.

2. Your pattern will give you a needle size and tension for 4in (10cm). Use this to work out how many stitches you need to cast on, then join to work in the round.

3. Knit until you reach the point where you would like your thumbhole to sit, then work as follows:
   Thumbhole rnd 1: K2, cast off 1½in (4cm) worth of sts, k to end of rnd.
   Thumbhole rnd 2: K2, cast on the same number of sts you cast off on the previous rnd, k to end of rnd.

4. Continue knitting until your mitt is as long as you want it to be, then cast off.

5. Measure the number of stitches and rows you get to 4in (10cm) and compare to your pattern.

6. Wash your swatch mitt in the way you plan to wash your garment (you may find instructions on the yarn band but for all but the most delicate fibres I tend to use the hand-wash cycle of my washing machine), then measure your stitches and rows again.

7. You may want to knit a second mitt – or mix and match with other swatches.

These swatch mitts were knitted in Artyarns Merino Cloud, a blend of 80% Merino wool and 20% cashmere, in shades 172 Tutti Frutti and 160 Virgin Islands, on 3.75mm needles. An added benefit of these particular mitts was that I was able to confirm that colours from the two shades wouldn't run into each other when I washed my finished garment.

Talking 'bout my inspiration

My journey to seamless knitting has been inspired and influenced by a great many brilliant designers, some of whom I'd love to introduce to you here.

DEBBIE STOLLER

Debbie's series of *Stitch 'n Bitch* books took my knitting to a whole new level. I'd always had a sense that knitting should be funky, quirky and fun – but that never seemed to be borne out in the dreary pattern leaflets I found in yarn shops. But that's exactly what Debbie did in *Stitch 'n Bitch*. I knitted my first cardigan in one piece – *Fairly Easy Fair Isle* by Kate Watson from *Stitch 'n Bitch Nation* – and I was away.

JARED FLOOD

Photographer, designer and Brooklyn Tweed founder Jared Flood blew my mind with his *Smokin'* jacket in *Son of Stitch 'n Bitch* – I simply couldn't believe I could work the saddle shoulder shaping in one piece! Since then Jared has moved on to far more complex and intricate designs for his beautiful US-grown and milled wools, and he continues to be an inspiration.

ERIKA KNIGHT

Punk knitwear design legend Erika Knight brings her distinctively unconventional approach to all her pieces, which now combine this anti-establishment punk ethos with a restrained elegance and glamour, and are always stylishly presented and beautifully photographed. Apart from being an amazing designer Erika has always been really supportive of me and my work, which means a lot.

BRISTOL IVY

During the 2020 lockdown I was privileged to attend a brilliant lecture by Bristol at US magazine *Vogue Knitting*'s Virtual Knitting Live event, and have also been lucky enough to read her two *Knitting Outside the Box* books and even interview her for *Knitting* magazine. I came out of that lecture with a burning desire to tear up everything I'd ever learned and start over, knitting from a place I'd never knitted before.

ELIZABETH ZIMMERMANN

No one writes about knitting quite like Elizabeth Zimmermann, and her book *Knitting Without Tears* is one I go back to time and again. Elizabeth was a pioneer of knitting in the round, and I imagine that many of the designers who have inspired me were inspired by her in their turn. I also always use her EZ method of calculating sweater sizes when I'm designing – so this book wouldn't be here without her.

ÅSA TRICOSA

I took part in Richmond yarn boutique Tribe Yarns' virtual knit-along (KAL) to make Swedish designer Åsa Tricosa's signature *Ziggurat* sweater during a time of semi-pandemic lockdown. This jumper is knitted from the top down to fit the maker perfectly, and its set-in sleeves are a thing of beauty. The KAL also introduced me to Japanese short rows and inspired the seamless pockets and linings I've included here.

Tools and materials

There are just a couple of things you need to start knitting: sticks and string. But a few others things might come in handy too...

EQUIPPED FOR THE JOB

1. Circular needles

These come in materials including wood, metal, carbon fibre, plastic and more. They can either be fixed, or part of a set of interchangeable needles in different sizes. My favourites are wood as they're lightweight and warm in your hands, and I absolutely love my KnitPro Ginger interchangeable set. You can use these for knitting any circumference, with extra-long cords for very wide knits and using the magic loop method for small circumferences. You can also use circular needles to knit back and forth, which is good for your back, shoulders and wrists as the weight of the project then sits in your lap.

2. Double-pointed needles

Sets of double-pointed needles work well for small circumferences. They tend to come in sets of five, and stitches are spread across two, three or four needles and then knitted with another needle. These are my KnitPro Zings, which are made of lightweight metal. Because DPNs are often very small, bamboo ones can sometimes snap so I prefer metal in this instance. Be careful not to sit on them though!

3. Scissors

A good pair of scissors is essential. I love these stork embroidery scissors as they're sharp but small and lightweight, which makes them nice and portable.

4. Sewing needles

I know, I know, I said there would be no sewing but it's still useful to have some large-eyed, blunt-ended needles for weaving in ends, threading yarn through live stitches to fasten off and for grafting.

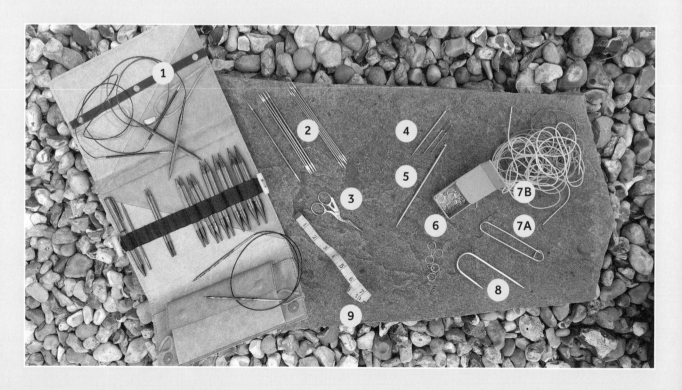

5. Crochet hook

This book doesn't really use crochet but a crochet hook is handy for picking up stitches. It's also used for making little bobbles in the *Force field* cardigan on page 64, and for provisional cast-ons.

6. Stitch markers

I find these particularly useful when knitting in the round as it's not always as easy to see where you are as it is when you're knitting back and forth. Many of the patterns in this book are built around stitch markers to save you counting stitches all the time. It's handy to have markers that are rings of various sizes and ones that open and close like tiny safety pins. These ones are Cocoknits' precious metal stitch markers, which were a treat to myself, but they can be as inexpensive as you like and you can even make your own from pieces of scrap yarn.

7. Stitch holders

Many of the patterns in this book call for stitches to be put on hold while other sections are worked. Stitch holders can be large safety pins (A), ordinary safety pins if there aren't too many stitches, or simply scrap yarn. Flexible stitch holders (B) are incredibly useful as they make it much easier to try on a garment while you work, and they're super easy to use. Those pictured are from online shop Knit + Living, but I've also had some brilliant ones from London yarn boutique Beautiful Knitters.

8. Cable needle

This cable needle is in a U shape, but they come in many different shapes and sizes and any work well for cabling. I have lots but I always lose them.

9. Measuring tape

Essential for measuring! Most have both inches and centimetres marked.

FIBRE FESTIVAL

Perhaps the best thing about knitting is working with beautiful, colourful yarns. These come in all sorts of fibres, but I tend to prefer working with natural ones. Some yarns are pure, like Cascade Magnum, a pure roving wool from Merino sheep, which have pretty much the softest fleece of all sheep (A). Others are blends. Rico's Superba Alpaca Luxury Sock (B) blends wool and alpaca fibre with polyamide, to give the socks softness and strength. If you knitted socks in pure wool they would get holes straight away. Rowan's Tweed Haze (C) blends mohair, alpaca, polyamide, cotton and polyester. Mohair and alpaca give softness and a fluffy halo, while cotton and manmade fibres add strength and resilience.

You can create your own blends. In the knitting bag you can see Lang Yarns Merino 150, a pure Merino wool, held together with Lang Yarns Alpaca Superlight (D), which blends alpaca with nylon and Merino wool. Working the smooth Merino together with the warm but extremely lightweight alpaca-dominated yarn creates a marled effect and gives a fluffy halo to the finished knit.

Yarns come in all shapes and sizes. If your yarn comes in a ball like Rowan Tweed Haze (C) or the Lang Yarns ones (D), you can just pick them up and start knitting. However, if it comes in a hank like this blue yarn (E), you will need to wind it before you start. To do this, carefully open out the hank into a big loop and slip it on to a swift or across the backs of two high-backed chairs, so it is held open but not taut. Cut the ties holding the yarn together with care, and then you can use a ball winder to wind it into cakes, like the Cascade Magnum here (A), or you can use your hands to wind it into a ball.

Get around

Get used to no-sew
knitting with some quick
and easy accessories.

Sown seeds

Tiny wheat sheaves are scattered across the body of this slouchy beanie, knitted from the bottom up and anchored with a twisted rib brim.

SIZE
Brim circumference: 15¾in (40cm)
Length: 8¾in (22cm)

YOU WILL NEED
Rico Luxury Hand-dyed Happiness
100% extra-fine Merino wool
(approx 427yd/390m per 100g)
1 x 100g hank in 001 Ecru-Blue
4mm circular or double-
    pointed needles
Stitch marker

Note: Yarn amounts given are based on average requirements and are approximate.

TENSION
24 sts and 34 rnds to 4in (10cm) over st st.
Use larger or smaller needles if necessary to obtain correct tension.

WHEAT SHEAF PATTERN
Worked over 14 sts and 16 rnds
Rnd 1: Knit.
Rnd 2 and every alt rnd: Knit.
Rnds 3, 5 and 7: K2, yo, sk2po, yo, k9.
Rnd 9: Knit.
Rnds 11, 13 and 15: K9, yo, sk2po, yo, k2.
Rnd 16: Knit.
These 16 rnds form patt and are repeated.

HAT
Cast on 112 sts. Join to work in the round, taking care not to twist sts, and pm to mark beg of rnd.
Knit 1 rnd.
Rib rnd: (K1 tbl, p1) around.
Rep rib rnd until piece meas 2½in (6cm).

SET WHEAT SHEAF PATT
Work Wheat Sheaf Patt as set 8 times around, working 16-rnd patt a total of 3 times.
Knit 2 rnds.

SET CROWN DECREASES
Rnd 1: (K2tog, k8) to last 12 sts, k2tog, k10 (101 sts).
Rnd 2: K2tog, k to end (100 sts).

WHEAT SHEAF PATTERN

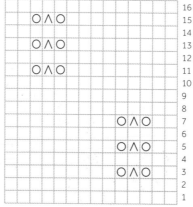

Rnd 3: (K2tog, k8) around (90 sts).
Rnd 4: Knit.
Rnd 5: (K2tog, k7) around (80 sts).
Rnd 6: Knit.
Rnd 7: (K2tog, k6) around (70 sts).
Rnd 8: (K2tog, k5) around (60 sts).
Rnd 9: (K2tog, k4) around (50 sts).
Rnd 10: (K2tog, k3) around (40 sts).
Rnd 11: (K2tog, k2) around (30 sts).
Rnd 12: (K2tog, k1) around (20 sts).
Rnd 13: (K2tog) around (10 sts).
Break yarn, thread through rem sts, pull tight then secure to fasten off.

TO FINISH
Weave in ends.

KEY

☐	knit
Ⓞ	yo
∧	sk2po

On the road

Take something cosy with you whenever you travel to keep your daily caffeine hit nice and warm. It'll help you remember your sustainable reusable mug too.

SIZE
Circumference bottom: 8½in (22cm)
Circumference top: 10¼in (26cm)
Length: 3in (8cm)

YOU WILL NEED
Cascade 220 Superwash Merino
100% superwash Merino wool (approx 220yd/200m per 100g)
Pictured in 28 Black, 25 White and 96 Molten Lava
4.5mm double-pointed or circular needles
Cable needle
Stitch markers

Note: Only small amounts of yarn are needed for this project. Finished weight of coffee cosy is 10g. Yarn amounts given are based on average requirements and are approximate.

TENSION
20 sts and 28 rows to 4in (10cm) over st st using 4.5mm needle. *Use larger or smaller needles if necessary to obtain correct tension.*

TIP
Wind off a ball of your main yarn (A) before starting as you will use two separate balls to work motif section.

COFFEE COSY
Using B, cast on 43 sts. Join to work in the round, taking care not to twist sts, and pm to mark beg of rnd.
Purl 1 rnd.
Change to A.
*Knit 1 rnd.
Purl 1 rnd.*
Change to B.
Rep from * to *.
Change to A.
Next rnd (inc): K2, m1L, k to last 2 sts, m1R, k2 (45 sts).

SET MOTIF SECTION
Rnd 1: Yo, k18, pm, work Heart Motif row 1 over next 9 sts, changing to a new ball of A after B section, pm, k to last st, ssk last st tog with yarn over at start of rnd, turn.
Rnd 2: With WS facing, yo, p to m, sm, work Heart Motif over next 9 sts, sm, p to last st, ptog last st with yarn over at start of rnd, turn.
Rnd 3: With RS facing, yo, k2, m1L, k to m, sm, work Heart Motif over next 9 sts, sm, k to last 2 sts, m1R, k1, ssk last st tog with yarn over at start of rnd, turn (47 sts).
Rnds 4 and 6: As rnd 2.
Rnd 5: With RS facing, yo, k to m, sm, work Heart Motif over next 9 sts, sm, k to last st, ssk last st tog with yo at start of rnd, turn.
Rnd 7: As rnd 3 (49 sts).
Rnds 8 and 9: As rnds 4 and 5.
Heart Motif is now complete.

Break B and return to just one ball of A.
Next rnd (inc): Work inc rnd again (51 sts).

SET BORDER
Change to B.
*Knit 1 rnd.
Purl 1 rnd.*
Change to A.
Rep from * to *.
Change to B.
Knit 1 rnd.
Cast off pwise.

TO FINISH
Weave in ends carefully. Wrap in a wet tea towel and press under a hot iron.

TRAVEL BUG
Taking your knitting on holiday? Use wooden needle tips instead of metal ones to avoid them being picked up on security scanners!

HEART MOTIF   **KEY**

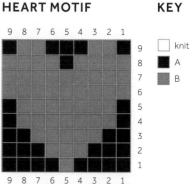

	knit
■	A
▨	B

Lovecats

I bought this yarn to match the little black and white kittens who joined our family recently and have been such lovely additions to the household, bringing great joy and much love. The cowl and mitts are nearly as soft and cosy as the kittens themselves, but they don't purr (or scratch the furniture).

SIZE

To fit: Average adult
Mitts circumference: 6¼in (16cm)
Mitts length: 9¾in (25cm)
Cowl circumference: 25¼in (64cm)

YOU WILL NEED

CaMaRose Snefnug 55% alpaca, 35% cotton, 10% extra fine Merino wool (approx 120yd/110m per 50g)
2 x 50g balls in 7325 Sort (A)
2 x 50g balls in 7811 Snehvid (B)
5mm and 5.5mm circular or
    double-pointed needles
Stitch markers
Scrap yarn

Note: Yarn amounts given are based on average requirements and are approximate.

TENSION

11 sts and 24 rnds to 10cm over patt using 5.5mm needles.
Use larger or smaller needles if necessary to obtain correct tension.

TIP

To avoid jogs in your stripes, when changing colour twist yarns at the back of the work. When you have worked one full rnd in the new shade, slip the first stitch of the next rnd pwise.

CHEVRON PATTERN

Worked over 12 sts and 2 rnds
Rnd 1: K1, ssk, k3, m1L, k1, m1R, k3, k2tog.
Rnd 2: Knit.
These 2 rnds form patt and are repeated.

LEFT MITT

Using 5mm needles and A, cast on 24 sts. Join to work in the round, taking care not to twist sts, and pm to mark beg of rnd.
Rib rnd: (K1, p1) around.
Rep rib rnd until piece meas 2cm (¾in)
SET CHEVRON PATT
Change to 5.5mm needles.
Work 2 rnds in Chevron Patt.
Change to B.
Work 4 rnds in Chevron Patt.
Change to A.
Work 4 rnds in Chevron Patt.
Rep last 8 rnds 2 more times, then work 4 more rnds in Chevron Patt in B.
Piece meas approx 7½in (19cm).
Change to A.

Work 1 rnd in Chevron Patt.**
SET THUMBHOLE
Next rnd: Patt to last 4 sts, patt across last 4 sts using scrap yarn, slip sts back to LH needle and work again using A.
***HAND**
Work 2 rnds in Chevron Patt.
Change to B and work 4 rnds in Chevron Patt.
Change to A and work 2 rnds in Chevron Patt.
Change to 5mm needles and rep rib rnd as above 6 times. Cast off.

THUMB

Using 5mm needles, pick up 4 sts at bottom of scrap yarn, 1 st in gap between bottom and top, 4 sts along top of scrap yarn and 1 st in gap between top and bottom (10 sts). Remove scrap yarn.
Work rib rnd as above for 6 rnds.
Cast off.

RIGHT MITT

Work as Left Mitt to **.

CHART

12	11	10	9	8	7	6	5	4	3	2	1	
/				↱		↰				↘		2
												1

12 11 10 9 8 7 6 5 4 3 2 1

KEY

☐	knit
↘	ssk
/	k2tog
↰	m1L
↱	m1R

SET THUMBHOLE
Next rnd: Patt 12, work next 4 sts using scrap yarn, slip sts back to LH needle and work again using A, patt to end. Work as Left Mitt from *** to end.

COWL
Using 5mm needle and B, cast on 72 sts. Join to work in the rnd, taking care not to twist sts, and pm to mark beg of rnd.
Rib rnd: (K1, p1) around.
Rep rib rnd 5 more times.

SET CHEVRON PATT
Change to 5.5mm needles.
Work 2 rnds in Chevron Patt.
Change to A.
Work 4 rnds in Chevron Patt.
Change to B.
Work 4 rnds in Chevron Patt.
Rep last 8 rnds 3 more times.
Piece meas approx 7in (18cm)
Change to A.
Work 4 more rnds in Chevron Patt.
Change to B.
Work 2 more rnds in Chevron Patt.

SET RIB
Change to 5mm needles.
Work rib rnd as above for 6 rnds.
Cast off.

TO FINISH
Weave in ends.
Block.

BREATHING SPACE
Simple stitch patterns like the chevrons in this design can be a great way to bring mindfulness to your craft by practising a simple breathing exercise while you knit. Start with your knitting in your lap, close your eyes and take three long, deep breaths before you begin, feeling your belly expand as you breathe in and contract as you empty it all out – you may want to sigh out loud, as this can feel very relaxing. Now, working in time with your own knitting speed, try to match slow inhales and exhales to your stitches, for example:

1. Breathe in and k3.
2. Breathe out and work m1L, k1, m1R.
3. Breathe in and k3.
4. Breathe out and work k2tog, k1, ssk.

At the end of your knitting session, before you rush off to the business of life, finish with three more deep breaths.

Love a cuppa

Who doesn't love a cuppa? This quick and easy stranded colourwork tea cosy will keep your teapot snug and your drink warm as long as you need it, and it's served with lots and lots of love.

SIZE
Circumference: 19in (48cm)
Height: 8in (20cm)

YOU WILL NEED
Cascade Magnum 100% Peruvian Highland wool (approx 123yd/112.5m per 250g)
1 x 250g hank in 9431 Regal Red (A)
1 x 250g hank in 9478 Cotton Candy (B)
10mm circular or double-pointed needles
Extra 10mm needle for three-needle cast off
Stitch markers

Note: Only small amounts of yarn are used. Total project weighs 95g. Yarn amounts given are based on average requirements and are approximate.

TENSION
8 sts and 13 rnds to 4in (10cm) over st st.
Use larger or smaller needles if necessary to obtain correct tension.

PATTERN NOTE
It's easy to adapt this little tea cosy to suit a bigger pot: simply cast on however many extra stitches you would like, and work them in A on either side of the Chart pattern.

TEA COSY
Using B, cast on 40 sts and join to work in the round, taking care not to twist sts. Pm to mark beg of rnd and after 20 sts to mark halfway point.
Purl 1 rnd.
Change to A.
Knit 8 rnds.

SET CHART
Next rnd: *K1, work row 1 of Chart across next 18 sts, k1; sm, rep from * once more.
This rnd sets position of Chart. Cont as set until you have worked all 6 rows of Chart.

Break B and cont in A only.
Knit 3 rnds.

SET DECREASES
Next rnd (dec): *K1, ssk, k to 3 sts before m, k2tog, k1; sm, rep from * once more (36 sts).
Rep dec rnd 6 more times (12 sts).

THREE-NEEDLE CAST OFF
Turn Tea Cosy inside out so the WS is facing.
Distribute the rem 12 sts evenly over 2 needles so there are 6 sts on each needle.
Using a third needle, work three-needle cast off over all sts.
Fasten off.

TO FINISH
Weave in ends.
Wrap in a wet tea towel and press under a hot iron.

TEA COSY CHART

KEY
□ knit
▨ A
▨ B

Rows: 1 2 3 4 5 6
Columns: 18 17 16 15 14 13 12 11 10 9 8 7 6 5 4 3 2 1

Refuge

I take my knitting with me everywhere. It provides an escape from boredom, if I find myself waiting around for something, and a refuge from anxiety, as the rhythmic movement of my hands soothes me. The fact that I'm doing something useful gives me a happy dopamine hit, and the distraction from whatever is bothering me can be enough to drive the fear into the background. This handy bag will hang comfortably off your wrist so you can retreat into your current knitting project whenever and wherever you need to.

SIZE
Width: 8¾in (22cm)
Length excluding handles: 9in (23cm)
Length including handles: 13in (33cm)

YOU WILL NEED
BC Garn Hamelton 1
100% Argentinian wool dyed in Italy
(approx 110yd/100m per 50g)
1 x 50g ball in 113 Camel Marled (A)
1 x 50g ball in 110 Turquoise (B)
1 x 50g ball in 115 Gold (C)
1 x 50g ball in 104 Light Red (D)
4mm circular or double-pointed
    needles
Stitch markers
Stitch holders

Note: Yarn amounts given are based on average requirements and are approximate.

TENSION
22 sts and 28 rows to 4in (10cm) over st st Fairisle patt after blocking using 4mm or 5mm needle (see box).
Use larger or smaller needles if necessary to obtain correct tension.

GET YOUR TENSION RIGHT
Stranded colourwork can affect your tension. I use a needle 1mm larger than the main needles to make sure my tension stays correct. Be sure to check your tension and if, like me, you find your work is tighter over the colourwork then use a 5mm needle for this section.

PERFECT FINISH
Blocking is essential when working stranded colourwork. For this project you can cover the bag with a wet tea towel and then use an ordinary iron to steam it.

BAG
Using A, cast on 96 sts using Judy's Magic Cast On. Pm to mark beg of rnd. Knit 2 rnds.

SET CHART
Work in Fairisle patt from Chart, working patt rep 8 times around and working through all 55 rnds.
Strand yarns not in use across the back of work, taking care not to pull tightly as this will affect your tension. Break yarns where it is more convenient.
Change to 4mm needle and cont in C only for remainder of project.
Next rnd: Knit.
Next rnd: Purl.
Rep last 2 rnds 2 more times.

DIVIDE FOR HANDLES
Next rnd: K to last 5 sts, cast off 10 sts, k39, then slip first 38 sts just worked on to a holder for second handle leaving 1 st on needle, cast off 10 sts, cont on rem 38 sts only for first handle.
**Next row (WS): K3, p to last 3 sts, k3.
Next row (RS): K3, ssk, k to last 5 sts, k2tog, k3 (36 sts).
Rep last 2 rows 4 more times (28 sts).
Cont as foll:
Row 1 (WS): K3, p to last 3 sts, k3.
Row 2: Knit.

Row 3: K3, p to last 3 sts, k3.

Row 4: K3, ssk, k to last 5 sts, k2tog, k3 (34 sts).

Rep last 4 rows until 20 sts rem.

Rep rows 1 and 2 a further 4 times, then work row 1 again. **

Slip sts to a holder.

SECOND HANDLE

With WS facing, rejoin yarn to sts for second handle and rep from ** to **. Return first handle sts to needle and join and cast off at the same time using the three-needle cast off.

TO FINISH

Weave in ends. Wrap in a wet tea towel and press under a hot iron.

ON THE MOVE

Knitting when you're out and about can garner some strange looks and comments – but who cares? Some knitters love to knit in unusual places – you can find some of them on Instagram using the hashtag #placesyoucanknit

CHART

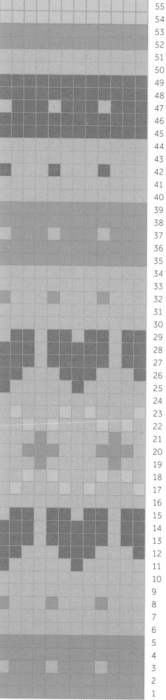

12 11 10 9 8 7 6 5 4 3 2 1

55
54
53
52
51
50
49
48
47
46
45
44
43
42
41
40
39
38
37
36
35
34
33
32
31
30
29
28
27
26
25
24
23
22
21
20
19
18
17
16
15
14
13
12
11
10
9
8
7
6
5
4
3
2
1

12 11 10 9 8 7 6 5 4 3 2 1

KEY

☐ knit

▢ A

▢ B

▢ C

▢ D

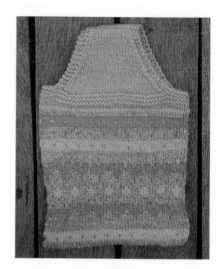

Laburnum

In spite of its less poetic name, Fishtail Lace creates as pretty and floral a pattern as the Laburnum Stitch rib it is partnered with here. This lacy hat and mitts set is perfect for springtime.

SIZES
HAT
Brim circumference (stretchy):
15¾in (40cm)
Height: 9¾in (25cm)
MITTS
Cuff circumference (stretchy):
5in (13cm)
Length: 9in (23cm)

YOU WILL NEED
Kettle Yarn Co Northiam DK
100% British Bluefaced Leicester
(approx 128yd/117m per 50g skein)
HAT
1 x 50g skein in Caspian (A)
MITTS
1 x 50g skein in Samphire (B)
Stitch holder or scrap yarn
FOR BOTH
3.5mm and 4mm double-pointed
   or circular needles
Stitch markers

Note: Yarn amounts given are based on average requirements and are approximate.

TENSION
22 sts and 30 rnds to 4in (10cm) over st st using 4mm needles.
27 sts and 30 rnds to 4in (10cm) over Laburnum Stitch using 3.5mm needles. Each Fishtail Lace rep (using 4mm needles) is approx 2in (5cm) wide x 1¼in (3cm) long.
Use larger or smaller needles if necessary to obtain correct tension.

TIP
When working rnd 3 of Laburnum Stitch, take the yarn to the front, slip the next st pwise, then take the yarn to the back, wrapping the slipped stitch. Knit the next 2 sts together and pass the wrapped slipped stitch over. A double yarn over compensates for this double decrease so the stitch count remains the same.

LABURNUM STITCH
Worked over 5 sts and 4 rnds
Rnds 1 and 2: (P2, k3) to end.
Rnd 3: (P2, yf, sl1p, yb, k2tog, psso, yo twice) to end.
Rnd 4: (P2, k1, kfb into double yo) to end.

FISHTAIL LACE
Worked over 9 sts and 8 rnds
Rnd 1: (Yo, k3, sk2po, k3, yo) to end.
Rnd 2 and all alt rnds: Knit.
Rnd 3: (K1, yo, k2, sk2po, k2, yo, k1) to end.
Rnd 5: (K2, yo, k1, sk2po, k1, yo, k2) to end.
Rnd 7: (K3, yo, sk2po, yo, k3) to end.
Rnd 8: Knit.

LABURNUM STITCH

5	4	3	2	1	
↘			•	•	4
∘∘		∧	•	•	3
			•	•	2
			•	•	1

5 4 3 2 1

KEY

☐	knit
•	purl
╱	k2tog
∧	yf, sl1p, yb, k2tog, psso
∘∘	yo twice
↘	kfb

FISHTAIL LACE

9	8	7	6	5	4	3	2	1	
									8
		O	∧	O					7
									6
		O		∧		O			5
									4
	O			∧			O		3
									2
O				∧				O	1

9 8 7 6 5 4 3 2 1

KEY

☐	knit
O	yo
∧	sk2po

HAT

Using 3.5mm needles and A, cast on 90 sts. Join to work in the round, taking care not to twist sts, and pm to mark beg of rnd.

SET LABURNUM STITCH

Rnd 1: Work Laburnum Stitch patt 18 times around.

Rnd 1 sets Laburnum Stitch. Cont as set until you have worked 6 full patt reps, ending after rnd 4.

SET FISHTAIL LACE

Change to 4mm needles.

Next rnd: (K10, pm) 8 times, k10.

Next rnd: (K1, work Fishtail Lace patt, sm) 8 times, work Fishtail Lace patt once more.

This rnd sets position of Fishtail Lace patt. Cont as now set until you have worked 6 full reps of Fishtail Lace patt, ending after rnd 8.

Knit 1 rnd, removing markers.

SET CROWN DECS

Rnd 1: (K7, k2tog) around (80 sts).
Rnd 2: Knit.
Rnd 3: (K6, k2tog) around (70 sts).
Rnd 4: Knit.

Rnd 5: (K5, k2tog) around (60 sts).
Rnd 6: (K4, k2tog) around (50 sts).
Rnd 7: (K3, k2tog) around (40 sts).
Rnd 8: (K2, k2tog) around (30 sts).
Rnd 9: (K1, k2tog) around (20 sts).
Rnd 10: (K2tog) around (10 sts).
Break yarn, thread through rem 10 sts and pull tight to fasten off.

LEFT MITT

Using 3.5mm needles and B, cast on 35 sts. Join to work in the round, taking care not to twist sts, and pm to mark beg of rnd.

Rnd 1: Work Laburnum Stitch patt 7 times around.

This rnd sets Laburnum Stitch.

Cont as set until you have worked 7 full patt reps, then work rnds 1 and 2 once more.

SET MAIN PATTERN AND THUMBHOLE INCREASES

Change to 4mm needles.

Knit 1 rnd, inc 1 st (36 sts).**

Rnd 1: K5, pm1, work rnd 1 of Fishtail Lace patt, k to last st, yo, pm2, k1, yo (38 sts).

***Rnd 2:** Knit.

Rnd 3: K to m1, sm, work rnd 3 of Fishtail Lace patt, k to m2, yo, sm, k1, yo, k to end (40 sts).

Rnd 4: Knit.

Rep rnds 3 and 4 four more times, but working through Fishtail Lace patt as now set (48 sts).

Rnd 5: K to m1, sm, work Fishtail Lace patt over next 9 sts, k to 2 sts before m2, k2tog, yo, sm, k1, yo, ssk, k to end.

Rnd 6: Knit.

Rep rnds 5 and 6 until you have worked 3 full reps of Fishtail Lace patt.****

Slip last 13 sts of rnd to a holder for thumbhole.

*****Cont on rem 35 sts only.

Next rnd: K to m, sm, work Fishtail Lace patt over next 9 sts, k to end.

Cont as now set for 1 full patt rep.

Knit 1 rnd.

Change to 3.5mm needles.

Next rnd: Work Laburnum Stitch patt 7 times around.

Cont as now set, working 2 full reps of Laburnum Stitch patt, then work rows 1 and 2 once more.

Cast off loosely in patt.

THUMB

Rejoin 13 held sts for thumbhole to needles, pick up and k2 sts from side of hand (15 sts).

Work 1 rep of Laburnum Stitch patt 3 times around, then work rows 1 and 2 again.

Cast off loosely in patt.

RIGHT MITT

Work as Left Mitt to **.

Rnd 1: K5, pm1, sm, work rnd 1 of Fishtail Lace patt, k5, yo, pm2, k1, yo, k to end (38 sts).

Work as Left Mitt from *** to ****.

Next rnd: K to m1, sm, work Fishtail Lace patt over next 9 sts, k5, slip next 13 sts to holder for thumbhole, k to end.

Work as Left Mitt from ***** to end.

TO FINISH

Weave in ends.

Block according to yarn band instructions to open out lace pattern.

See the light

To the uninitiated, sock knitting looks incredibly hard. This simple pattern is designed to help you see the light: they're actually as simple as can be! These socks are knitted with an afterthought heel so there are no short rows to worry about, and you can knit them from the top down or from the toe up, depending on how you feel. Once you've mastered the plain sock, either in a solid colour or with a contrast toe, heel and cuff, why not try the Daisy Rib version? It's exactly the same sock, but with a fancy Japanese-style flower rib. Daisies are such a happy flower, seeking out the light, and I created this version for my own daughter Daisy, who has been a budding fashionista since before she could walk.

SIZES

To fit: 0-12mths[12-24mths:2-4yrs: 4-7yrs:8-11yrs:adult S:adult M:adult L]

Ankle circumference (stretchy):
4[4¼:4¾:5¼:5½:6¼:7:8]in
(10[11:12:13:14:16:18:20]cm)

Foot length: 3½[4:4¾:6:8:9:10¼:11]in
(9[10:12:15:20:23:26:28]cm)
(adjustable)

Figures in square brackets refer to larger sizes: where there is only one set of figures this applies to all sizes.

YOU WILL NEED

Rico Superba Alpaca Luxury Sock
62% wool, 23% polyamide, 15% alpaca
(approx 340yd/310m per 100g)
2.5mm and 3mm double-pointed
    or circular needles
Stitch markers
Scrap yarn

Note: One ball will make one pair of socks up to size L, but most of these designs use much smaller amounts of yarn. Samples shown in shades 002 Pink, 004 Silver, 005 Grey, 006 Black and 007 Yellow.
Yarn amounts given are based on average requirements and are approximate.

TENSION

30 sts and 39 rnds to 4in (10cm) over st st.
Daisy Rib patt meas 1¼in wide x 1¾in long (3 x 4cm).
Use larger or smaller needles if necessary to obtain correct tension.

PATTERN NOTES

Although the ribbed version of the socks appears a little tighter, it is so stretchy that this will not affect the finished measurements.
For contrast socks work as plain and Daisy Rib socks, but work cuff rib, toe and afterthought heel in a contrast shade.

PLAIN SOCKS

PLAIN SOCKS FROM THE TOP DOWN (MAKE 2)
Using 2.5mm needles, cast on 30[34:42:46:50:58:66:74] sts.
Join to work in the round, taking care not to twist sts, and pm to mark beg of rnd and after 15[17:21:23:25:29:33:37] sts to mark halfway point.

CUFF
Rib rnd: (K1, p1) around.

Rep rib rnd until cuff meas ¼[¼:½:¾:1:1:1:1]in (1[1:1.5:2:2.5:2.5:2.5:2.5]cm).

LEG
Change to 3mm needles.
Cont in st st (knit every rnd) until leg (including cuff) meas 2[2½:2¾:4:6:6¾:7½:8¼]in (5[6:7:10:15:17:19:21]cm) or desired length.

SET AFTERTHOUGHT HEEL
Next rnd: K to halfway point marker, use scrap yarn to k to end. Slip sts worked in scrap yarn back to LH needle and work again using main yarn, ending at end of rnd.

FOOT
Cont in st st in the rnd until foot meas approx 2½[2½:2¾:3½:4¾:4¾:4¾:4¾]in (6[6:7:9:12:12:12:12]cm) or 1¼[1½:2:2¼:3¼:4¼:5½:6¼]in (3[4:5:6:8:11:14:16]cm) less than desired length.

**SET TOE DECREASES
SIZES 1-4 ONLY
Dec rnd: *K1, ssk, k to 3 sts before m, k2tog, k1, sm; rep from * to end (dec 4).
Knit 1 rnd.
Rep last 2 rnds 0[1:2:3] more times.
Then rep dec rnd every rnd until 14[14:18:18] sts rem.

SIZES 5-8 ONLY

Dec rnd: *K1, ssk, k to 3 sts before m, k2tog, k1, sm; rep from * to end (dec 4).

Knit 2 rnds.

Rep last 3 rnds 1[1:2:3] more times. Then rep dec rnd every alt rnd until 22 sts rem.

ALL SIZES

Graft sts tog and fasten off.

AFTERTHOUGHT HEEL

Using 2.5mm needles, pick up 15[17:21:23:25:29:33:37] sts on each side of scrap yarn and 1 st in gap at each side, then carefully remove scrap yarn.

32[36:44:48:52:60:68:76] sts.

Pm to mark beg of rnd and after 16[18:22:24:26:30:34:38] sts to mark halfway point.

Change to 3mm needles.

Next rnd: *K1, ssk, k to halfway m, sm; rep from * once more. 30[34:42:46:50:58:66:74] sts. Now work as for toe decreases to end.

PLAIN SOCKS FROM THE TOE UP (MAKE 2)

Using 3mm needles and Judy's Magic Cast On, cast on 14[14:18:18:22:22:22:22] sts. Pm to mark beg of rnd and after 7[7:9:9:11:11:11:11] sts for halfway point.

TOE

Knit 1 rnd.

SIZES 1-4 ONLY

Inc rnd: *K1, kfb, k to 2 sts before m, kfb, k1, sm; rep from * to end (inc 4).

Rep inc rnd 2 more times. 26[26:30:30] sts.

Knit 1 rnd.

Rep last 2 rnds 1[2:3:4] more times. 30[34:42:46] sts.

SIZES 5-8 ONLY

Inc rnd: *K1, kfb, k to 2 sts before m, kfb, k1, sm; rep from * to end (inc 4).

Knit 1 rnd.

Rep last 2 rnds 4[6:7:8] more times. 42[50:54:58] sts.

Work inc rnd once more, then knit 2 rnds.

Rep last 3 rnds 1[1:2:3] more times. 50[58:64:74] sts.

ALL SIZES

30[34:42:46:50:58:66:74] sts.***

FOOT

Cont in st st in the rnd until foot meas approx 3[3¼:3¾:4¾:6¼:7:7½:8]in (7.5[8:9.5:12:16:18:19:20]cm) or ½[¾:1:1¼:1½:2:2¾:3¼]in (1.5[2:2.5:3:4:5:7:8]cm) less than desired length.

SET AFTERTHOUGHT HEEL

Next rnd: K to halfway point marker, use scrap yarn to k to end.

Slip sts worked in scrap yarn back to LH needle and work again using main yarn, ending at end of rnd.

LEG

Cont in st st until leg meas 1½[2:2¼:3¼:5:5¾:6½:7¼]in (4[5:5.5:8:12.5:14.5:16.5:18.5]cm) or ¼[¼:½:¾:1:1:1:1]in (1[1:1.5:2:2.5:2.5:2.5:2.5]cm) less than desired length.

CUFF

Change to 2.5mm needles.

Rib rnd: (K1, p1) around.

Rep rib rnd until cuff meas ¼[¼:½:¾:1:1:1:1]in (1[1:1.5:2:2.5:2.5:2.5:2.5]cm).

Cast off using a stretchy cast-off method.

AFTERTHOUGHT HEEL

Work as for top-down socks.

DAISY RIB SOCKS

DAISY RIB PATTERN
Worked over 11 sts and 16 rnds
Rnds 1-3: P2, (k1 tbl, p1) 4 times, p1.
Rnd 4: P2, k1 tbl, p1, cl3, p1, k1 tbl, p2.
Rnd 5: P2, k1 tbl, p1, k3, p1, k1 tbl, p2.
Rnd 6: P2, cl3, k1, cl3, p2.
Rnd 7: P2, k7, p2.

Rnd 8: P2, k2, cl3, k2, p2.
Rnd 9: As rnd 7.
Rnd 10: As rnd 6.
Rnd 11: P2, k1 tbl, p1 tbl, k3, p1 tbl, k1 tbl, p2.
Rnd 12: P2, k1 tbl, p1, cl3, p1, k1 tbl, p2.
Rnd 13: P2, k1 tbl, p1, k1, p1 tbl, k1, p1, k1 tbl, p2.
Rnds 14-16: As rnds 1-3.

DAISY RIB SOCKS FROM THE TOP DOWN (MAKE 2)
Using 2.5mm needles, cast on 30[34:42:46:50:58:66:74] sts.
Join to work in the round, taking care not to twist sts, and pm to mark beg of rnd and after 15[17:21:23:25:29:33:37] sts to mark halfway point.

CUFF
SIZES 1 AND 4 ONLY
Rib rnd: *(K1, p1) to 1 st before halfway point marker, k1; sm, rep from * once more.

SIZES 2, 3, 5, 6, 7 AND 8 ONLY
Rib rnd: *(P1, k1) to 1 st before halfway point marker, p1; sm, rep from * once more.

ALL SIZES
Rep rib rnd until cuff meas ¼[¼:½:¾:1:1:1:1]in (1[1:1.5:2:2.5:2.5:2.5:2.5]cm).

LEG
Change to 3mm needles.
SIZES 1 AND 2 ONLY
Next rnd: *K1, p1[2], work rnd 1 of Daisy Rib Patt over next 11 sts, p1[2], k1, sm; rep from * to end.
This rnd sets position of Daisy Rib Patt. Work rnds 1 and 2 once, then work rnds 1-16, then rep rnds 1 and 2 once more.

SET AFTERTHOUGHT HEEL
Next rnd: Patt to halfway point marker, use scrap yarn to k to end. Slip sts worked in scrap yarn back to LH needle and work again using main yarn, ending at end of rnd.

FOOT
Now work Daisy Rib Patt as for Leg across top of foot sts and k across sole sts until you have worked 20 rnds in patt.

SIZES 3-8 ONLY
Next rnd: *(K1, p1) 2[2:3:4:5:6] times, p1[2:1:1:1:1], work rnd 1 of Daisy Rib Patt over next 11 sts, p1[2:1:1:1:1],

(p1, k1) 2[2:3:4:5:6] times, sm; rep from * to end.

This rnd sets position of Daisy Rib Patt. Cont as now set, working through all rnds of Daisy Rib Patt 2[2:3:3:3:3] times.

SET AFTERTHOUGHT HEEL

Next rnd: Patt to halfway point marker, use scrap yarn to k to end. Slip sts worked in scrap yarn back to LH needle and work again using main yarn, ending at end of rnd.

FOOT

Next rnd: Patt to halfway point marker as set, k to end.

This rnd sets Daisy Rib Patt across top of foot and st st across sole. Cont as now set until you have worked 3 full reps of Daisy Rib Patt, ending with rnd 16.

ALL SIZES

Work as for plain sock from the top down from ** to end.

DAISY RIB SOCKS FROM THE TOE UP (MAKE 2)

Work as for plain socks from the toe up to ***.

FOOT

SIZES 1 AND 2 ONLY

Next rnd: *K1, p1[2], work rnd 1 of Daisy Rib Patt over next 11 sts, p1[2], k1, sm, k to end.

SIZES 3-8 ONLY

Next rnd: *(K1, p1) 2[2:3:4:5:6] times, p1[2:1:1:1:1], work rnd 1 of Daisy Rib Patt over next 11 sts, p1[2:1:1:1:1], (k1, p1) 2[2:3:4:5:6] times, sm, k to end.

ALL SIZES

This rnd sets foot patt.
Cont in patt as set as for top-down socks to afterthought heel.

SET AFTERTHOUGHT HEEL

Next rnd: K to halfway point marker, use scrap yarn to k to end.
Slip sts worked in scrap yarn back to LH

needle and work again using main yarn, ending at end of rnd.

LEG

SIZES 1 AND 2 ONLY

Next rnd: *K1, p1[2], work rnd 1 of Daisy Rib Patt over next 11 sts, p1[2], k1, sm; rep from * to end.

SIZES 3-8 ONLY

Next rnd: *(K1, p1) 2[2:3:4:5:6] times, p1[2:1:1:1:1], work rnd 1 of Daisy Rib Patt over next 11 sts, p1[2:1:1:1:1], (k1, p1) 2[2:3:4:5:6] times, sm; rep from * to end.

ALL SIZES

This rnd sets leg patt. Cont in patt as for toe-up socks to cuff.
Now work cuff as for top-down socks.

TO FINISH

Weave in ends and block according to yarn band instructions.

Get relaxed

Experience the joy of
knitting in the round with
these pleasing designs.

Shelter me

This warm but lightweight poncho brings the colour and feel of autumn to your wardrobe all year round, and wraps you up in sheltering warmth. The poncho is knitted in the round from the top down, starting with the ribbed cowl neck, increasing throughout the body and then finishing with short rows to give a longer back hem.

SIZE
Width at neckline: 13in (33cm)
Width at widest point: 28¼in (72cm)
Front length: 20½in (52cm)
Back length: 25½in (65cm)
Collar length: 9½in (24cm)

YOU WILL NEED
Rowan Tweed Haze 40% mohair, 39% alpaca, 10% polyamide, 8% cotton, 3% polyester (approx 131yd/120m per 50g ball)
5 x 50g balls in 557 Sunset
6mm circular needle
Stitch markers

Note: Yarn amounts given are based on average requirements and are approximate.

TENSION
14 sts and 20 rows to 4in (10cm) over st st.
Use smaller or larger needles if necessary to obtain correct tension.

LACE LADDER
Worked over 6 sts and 4 rnds
Rnd 1: P2, yo, ssk, p2.
Rnd 2: P2, k2, p2.
Rnd 3: P2, k2tog, yo, p2.
Rnd 4: As rnd 2.
These 4 rnds form patt and are repeated.

PONCHO
Cast on 124 sts. Join to work in the round, taking care not to twist sts, pm to mark beg of rnd and after 62 sts to mark halfway point.
Rib rnd: (K1, p1) around.
Rep rib rnd 6 more times.
Next rnd (dec): Rib to 1 st before halfway marker, remove marker, sk2po, pm, rib to last st, remove marker, sk2po, pm (120 sts).
Rib 3 rnds.
Rep last 4 rnds 6 more times, then work dec rnd once more (92 sts).
Rib 16 rnds straight.
Turn piece inside out so the WS becomes the RS and cont working in this way for the rest of the project. This is so that the neater side of the rib decreases will fall on the RS when the collar folds over.

SET BACK NECK ELEVATION
Worked using short rows.
Short row 1 (RS): K to halfway marker, sm, k1, w&t.

Short row 2 (WS): P to beg of rnd marker, sm, p1, w&t.
Short row 3: K to wrapped st, k wrap tog with wrapped st, w&t.
Short row 4: P to wrapped st, p wrap tog with wrapped st, w&t.
Short row 5: K to end of rnd.
Next rnd: Knit, working wraps tog with wrapped sts.

SET BODY PATT AND INCREASES
Rnd 1 (inc): K8, pm, m1L, k to 8 sts before end of rnd, m1R, pm, k to halfway marker, sm, k8, pm, m1L, pm, work Lace Ladder patt rnd 1 over next 6 sts, pm, k to last 14 sts, pm, work Lace Ladder patt rnd 1 over next 6 sts, pm, m1R, pm, k to end (96 sts).
Rnd 2: K to halfway marker, sm, k to inc marker, sm, k to first patt marker, sm, work Lace Ladder patt rnd 2 over next 6 sts, sm, k to next pattern marker, sm, work Lace Ladder patt rnd 2 over next 6 sts, k to end slipping markers.

LACE LADDER

6	5	4	3	2	1	
•	•			•	•	4
•	•	O	/	•	•	3
•	•			•	•	2
•	•	\	O	•	•	1

6 5 4 3 2 1

KEY

□	knit
•	purl
O	yo
/	k2tog
\	ssk

Rnd 3: K to inc marker, sm, m1L,
k to next inc marker, m1R, sm, k to next
inc marker slipping markers, sm, m1L,
k to first patt marker, sm, work rnd 3
of Lace Ladder patt, sm, k to next patt
marker, sm, work rnd 3 of Lace Ladder
patt, sm, k to inc marker, m1R, sm,
k to end (100 sts).

Rnd 4: As rnd 2, but working rnd 4 of
Lace Ladder patt.

These 4 rnds set position of Lace
Ladder patt and increases.

Cont as set, working inc rnd as foll:
Every alt rnd another 6 times (124 sts).
Every 4th rnd 19 times (200 sts).
Finish with rnd 4 of Lace Ladder patt.

SET SHORT-ROW HEM SHAPING

Short row 1 (RS): K to halfway marker,
k10, w&t.

Short row 2 (WS): P to halfway m, sm,
p to beg of rnd, sm, p10, w&t.

Short row 3: Slipping markers, k to
2 sts before wrapped st, w&t.

Short row 4: Slipping markers, p to
2 sts before wrapped st, w&t.

Rep last 2 rows 12 more times. 68 sts
rem between wraps after last wrap.

Next row (RS): K to end of rnd, working
wraps tog with wrapped sts as you
come to them.

Now cont in the rnd.

Knit 1 rnd, working any rem wraps tog
with wrapped sts.

Next rnd: (K1, p1) around.
Rep rib rnd 9 more times.
Cast off.

TO FINISH

Weave in ends. Block.

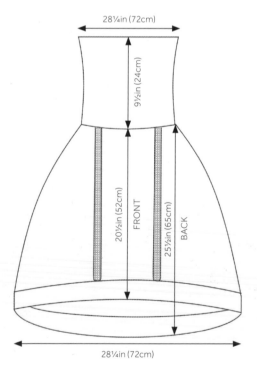

28¼in (72cm)

9½in (24cm)

20½in (52cm) FRONT

25½in (65cm) BACK

28¼in (72cm)

Entwined

Twisty braids adorn the back and sleeves of this cute, cropped jumper in a gorgeously rustic, organic Bavarian wool. Try it on as you go so it fits you perfectly, and finish off with a flattering scooped hemline at the back.

SIZES
To fit: UK 8-10[12-14:16-18:20-22: 24-26:28-30]

To fit full bust circumference:
33-35[37-39:41-43:46-48:51-54: 57-59]in (83-88[93-98:103-109: 116-123:130-137:144-151]cm)

Actual bust: 37½[42:47:52:58:63]in (95[106:119:133:147:161]cm)

Raglan seam length:
8¾[9½:10½:12½:13¼:15]in (22[24:27:32:34:38]cm)

Length back neck to hem (adjustable):
20¾[21:22:23¾:24¾:37¾]in (52.5[53:56:60.5:63:70.5]cm)

Length front underarm to hem (adjustable): 10¼in (26cm)

Sleeve length (adjustable):
17¾in (45cm)

Figures in square brackets refer to larger sizes: where there is only one set of figures this refers to all sizes.

YOU WILL NEED
Rauwerk Original 100% organic Bavarian wool
(approx 240yd/220m per 100g skein)
3[4:4:5:5:5] x 100g in Kies
5mm and 6mm circular needles
Cable needle
Stitch markers
Stitch holders or scrap yarn

Note: Yarn amounts given are based on average requirements and are approximate.

TENSION
14 sts and 22 rnds to 10cm over st st.
Use larger or smaller needles if necessary to obtain correct tension.

PATTERN NOTES
This raglan jumper is worked from the top down in the round, starting with the neck rib. There is a short-row elevation at the back neck, then the main pattern is set at the raglan sleeves and down the centre back. Once you have picked your yoke size, work body and sleeves to suit the length you want. The back hem is also given an optional curve using short rows. Where stitch markers are not mentioned, slip them. Size 1 is pictured on Caitlin, who is a UK size 6-8.

BRAID
Worked over 7 sts and 4 rnds
Rnds 1 and 3: (P1, k1 tbl) 3 times, p1.
Rnd 2: P1, Cr3L, p1, k1 tbl, p1.
Rnd 4: P1, k1 tbl, p1, Cr3R, p1.

SEAM 1
Worked over 5 sts and 5 rnds
Rnds 1, 2, 4 and 5: (P1, k1 tbl) twice, p1.
Rnd 3: P1, Cr3R, p1.

SEAM 2
Worked over 5 sts and 5 rnds
Rnds 1, 2, 4 and 5: (P1, k1 tbl) twice, p1.
Rnd 3: P1, Cr3L, p1.

JUMPER
Using 5mm needles cast on 69[73:73:73:77:77] sts. Join to work in the round, taking care not to twist sts, and pm to mark beg of rnd.

SET NECK RIB
Rib rnd: K2, pm, (p1, k1 tbl) 3 times, p1, pm (Braid Patt marker), (k2, p2) 15[16:16:16:17:17] times to end. Rep rib rnd 4 more times, slipping markers.

SET BACK NECK ELEVATION
Change to 6mm needle.
Set-up rnd: K2, sm, patt 7, sm,

BRAID

	7	6	5	4	3	2	1	
	•	⤬⤬			•	Q	•	4
	•	Q	•	Q	•	Q	•	3
	•	Q	•	⤬⤬		•	•	2
	•	Q	•	Q	•	Q	•	1
	7	6	5	4	3	2	1	

SEAM 1

	5	4	3	2	1	
	•	Q	•	Q	•	5
	•	Q	•	Q	•	4
	•	⤬⤬		•	•	3
	•	Q	•	Q	•	2
	•	Q	•	Q	•	1
	5	4	3	2	1	

SEAM 2

	5	4	3	2	1	
	•	Q	•	Q	•	5
	•	Q	•	Q	•	4
	•	⤬⤬		•	•	3
	•	Q	•	Q	•	2
	•	Q	•	Q	•	1
	5	4	3	2	1	

KEY

☐	knit
•	purl
Q	k tbl
⤬⤬	Cr3R
⤬⤬	Cr3L

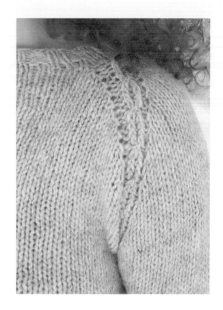

k8[9:9:9:10:10], pm1, k6, pm2,
k29[31:31:31:33:33], pm3, k6, pm4,
k to end.

Short row 1: Patt to m2, k1, w&t.

Short row 2: P to Braid Patt marker,
sm, (k1, p1 tbl) 3 times, k1, sm, p to m3,
p1, w&t.

Short row 3: Knit.

SET MAIN PATTERN

Note: On first rnd work wrapped sts
tog with wraps as you come to them,
in patt.

Rnd 1: K2, sm, work rnd 1 of Braid Patt
over 7 sts, sm, k to m1, m1L, sm, work
rnd 1 of Seam 1 over 5 sts, m1R, k1,
m1L, sm2, work rnd 1 of Seam 2 over
next 5 sts, m1R, k to m3, m1L, sm,
work rnd 1 of Seam 1 over 5 sts, m1R,
k1, m1L, sm4, work rnd 1 of Seam 2
over next 5 sts, m1R, k to end (inc 8).
77[81:81:81:85:85] sts.

Rnd 2: K2, sm, work rnd 2 of Braid Patt
over 7 sts, sm, k to m1, sm, work rnd 2
of Seam 1 over 5 sts, k to m2, sm,
work rnd 2 of Seam 2 over 5 sts, k to
m3, work rnd 2 of Seam 1 over 5 sts,
k to m4, work rnd 2 of Seam 2 over
5 sts, k to end.

Rnd 3 (inc): K2, sm, work Braid Patt as
set over 7 sts, sm, *k to m, m1L, sm,
patt 5, m1R; rep from * 3 more times,
k to end (inc 8).
85[89:89:89:93:93] sts.

Rnd 4: K2, sm, work Braid Patt to m, sm,
*k to m, sm, patt 5; rep from * 3 more
times, k to end.
Rep rnds 3 and 4 another
8[13:18:18:28:28] times, ending with
rnd 4. 149[193:233:233:317:317] sts.
Work inc rnd again, then work
2[2:2:2:3:3] rnds straight.
Rep last 3[3:3:3:4:4] rnds a total of
9[7:6:9:4:8] times.
221[249:281:305:349:381] sts.

SIZES 1-4 ONLY

Work 1[2:2:3] rnds straight.

ALL SIZES

221[249:281:305:349:381] sts:
61[69:77:83:95:103] for back,
62[70:78:84:96:104] for front,
39[45:53:59:69:77] each sleeve plus
4 sets of 5 seam sts.

DIVIDE FOR BODY AND SLEEVES

Next rnd: Patt to m1, *sm, (k2tog)
twice, k to m2, remove m, k1, (k2tog)
twice, slip 45[51:59:65:75:83] sleeve

sts just worked to holder or scrap yarn,
cast on 5[5:6:9:7:10] sts*, k to m3; rep
from * to *, k to end. Pm at centre of
cast-on sts to mark side seams.
Now cont on rem
133[149:167:185:205:227] sts for body.

Next rnd: K2, sm, work Braid Patt
as set to m, sm, k to end,
dec 0[0:2:0:0:2] sts evenly.
133[149:165:185:205:225] sts.
Cont straight, working Braid Patt
between markers as set and rem sts
in st st (knit every rnd), until piece
meas approx 9½in (24cm) from
underarms, or 1in (2.5cm) less than
desired length, ending with rnd 1 or
3 of Braid Patt.

SHAPE BACK HEM

Short row 1: Patt to 5 sts before side
seam, w&t.

Short row 2: P to m, sm, (k1, p1 tbl)
3 times, k1, sm, p to 5 sts before side
seam, w&t.

Short row 3: Patt to 3 sts before
wrapped st, w&t.

Short row 4: Patt as set by short row
2 to 3 sts before wrapped st, w&t.
Rep short rows 3 and 4 once more.

Next rnd: Patt as set, working all wraps tog with wrapped sts.

SET RIB

Change to 5mm needle.

Next rnd: K2, sm, (p1, k1 tbl) 3 times, p1, sm, (k2, p2) to end.

Rep last rnd 4 more times.

Cast off using a stretchy method.

SLEEVES (MAKE 2)

Slip 45[51:59:65:75:83] held sleeve sts to 6mm needle, pick up and k6[6:8:10:10:10] sts across cast-on sts, pm after 1[1:1:2:1:2] sts to mark centre under sleeve, *(k2tog, k1) 3 times *, k to last 9[9:10:11:10:12] sts, rep from * to *, k to end. 45[51:61:69:79:87] sleeve sts.

Next rnd: Knit. First sleeve seam marker now marks beg of rnd.

Next rnd: Sm, (p1, k1 tbl) twice (row 1 of Seam Patt), p1, sm, k to end. This rnd sets Seam Patt under arm as foll: Work Seam Patt 1 between markers underarm for right sleeve and Seam Patt 2 under arm between markers for left sleeve, working first rnd above as rnd 1 of patt, and cont in patt as set to cuff.

Next rnd: Patt to m, k2tog, k to last 2 sts before m, ssk (dec 2).

Patt 6[6:4:3:3:2] rnds.

Cont in patt, rep last 7[7:5:4:4:3] rnds 4[7:10:14:19:23] more times. 35[35:39:39:39:39] sts.

Cont straight until sleeve meas 17in (43cm) or 1in (2.5cm) less than desired sleeve length, ending with rnd 2 or 5 of Seam Patt.

CUFF

Rib rnd: Sm, (p1, k1 tbl) twice, p1, sm, (k2, p2) to last 2 sts, k2.

Rep rib rnd 4 more times.

Cast off using a stretchy cast off.

TO FINISH

Weave in ends.

Block.

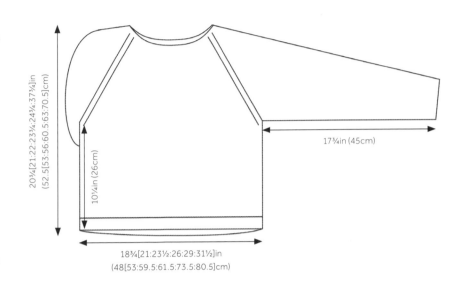

Calm waves

This is a really soothing knit with a lace pattern that reminds me of waves breaking on the shore the morning after a big storm has passed. You can either work this on a long circular needle using the magic loop method, or start off using dpns for the cuff and then change to straight needles for the body, which is worked back and forth. I call this garment a scarfigan, and it is knitted sideways from cuff to cuff. Although it has been designed as one size to fit all, it is easy to alter the length and width to suit your size and needs – just remember that if you make it bigger, you may need more yarn.

SIZE
Cuff circumference: 8¾in (22cm)
Cuff length: 15¾in (40cm)
Full length: 96in (244cm)
Width at widest point: 19in (48cm)

YOU WILL NEED
Rowan Brushed Fleece 65% wool, 30% alpaca, 5% polyamide (approx 125yd/115m per 50g)
5 x 50g balls in 273 Rock
6mm long circular needle
OR
6mm straight and double-pointed needles
Stitch markers

Note: Yarn amounts given are based on average requirements and are approximate.

TENSION
17 sts and 20 rows to 4in (10cm) over st st.
Wave patt meas 4¼in wide x 2¾in long (11 x 7cm)
Use larger or smaller needles if necessary to obtain correct tension.

WAVE 1
Worked over 14 sts and 14 rows
Row 1 (RS): P1, ssk, k7, yo, k1, yo, k2tog, p1.
Row 2 and all WS rows: K1, p12, k1.
Row 3: P1, ssk, k6, (yo, k1) twice, k2tog, p1.
Row 5: P1, ssk, k5, yo, k1, yo, k2, k2tog, p1.
Row 7: P1, ssk, k4, yo, k1, yo, k3, k2tog, p1.
Row 9: P1, ssk, k3, yo, k1, yo, k4, k2tog, p1.
Row 11: P1, ssk, k2, yo, k1, yo, k5, k2tog, p1.
Row 13: P1, ssk, (k1, yo) twice, k6, k2tog, p1.
Row 14: K1, p12, k1.

WAVE 1

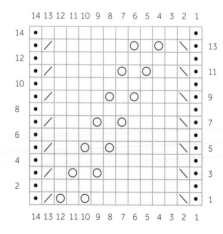

WAVE 2

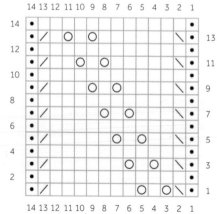

KEY

	RS: knit, WS: purl
•	RS: purl, WS: knit
\	ssk
/	k2tog
O	yo

WAVE 2

Worked over 14 sts and 14 rows

Row 1 (RS): P1, ssk, yo, k1, yo, k7, k2tog, p1.

Row 2 and all WS rows: K1, p12, k1.

Row 3: P1, ssk, (k1, yo) twice, k6, k2tog, p1.

Row 5: P1, ssk, k2, yo, k1, yo, k5, k2tog, p1.

Row 7: P1, ssk, k3, yo, k1, yo, k4, k2tog, p1.

Row 9: P1, ssk, k4, yo, k1, yo, k3, k2tog, p1.

Row 11: P1, ssk, k5, yo, k1, yo, k2, k2tog, p1.

Row 13: P1, ssk, k6, (yo, k1) twice, k2tog, p1.

Row 14: K1, p12, k1.

SCARFIGAN

Cast on 29 sts. Join to work in the round, taking care not to twist sts, and pm to mark beg of rnd.

RIGHT CUFF

Rib rnd: (K1, p1) to last st, k1.

Rep rib rnd 7 more times.

Cuff meas 2in (5cm).

Thumbhole rnd: K1, cast off 2 sts, rib to end.

Next rnd: K1, cast on 2 sts over cast-off sts, rib to end.

Cont in rib until cuff meas 15¾in (40cm).

SET BODY INCREASES

Note: Piece is worked back and forth from this point.

Row 1 (RS – inc): (K1, p1) twice, m1L, k to last 4 sts, m1R, (p1, k1) twice (31 sts).

Row 2 (WS): (P1, k1) twice, p to last 4 sts, (k1, p1) twice.

Rep last 2 rows 4 more times (39 sts).

SET MAIN PATTERN

Row 1 (RS – inc): (K1, p1) twice, work row 1 of Wave 1 over next 14 sts, pm, m1L, k3, m1R, pm, work row 1 of Wave 2 over next 14 sts, (p1, k1) twice (41 sts).

Row 2: (P1, k1) twice, work row 2 of Wave 2 to m, sm, p to m, sm, work row 2 of Wave 1, (k1, p1) twice.

Rows 1 and 2 set position of patterns and increases. Cont as set until you have worked 2 full patt reps, ending with row 14 (67 sts).

Now cont straight in patt as set until piece meas 75in (190cm), ending with row 14.

SET DECREASES

Row 1 (RS – dec): (K1, p1) twice, patt to m, sm, ssk, k to 2 sts before m, k2tog, sm, patt to last 4 sts, (p1, k1) twice.

Row 2: (P1, k1) twice, patt to m, sm, p to m, sm, patt to last 4 sts, (k1, p1) twice.

Rows 1 and 2 set patterns and decreases. Cont as set until you have worked 2 full patt reps in dec section, ending with row 14 (39 sts).

Next row (RS): (K1, p1) twice, ssk, k to last 6 sts, k2tog, (p1, k1) twice (dec 2).

Next row: (P1, k1) twice, p to last 4 sts, (k1, p1) twice.

Rep last 2 rows 4 more times (29 sts).

LEFT CUFF

Rejoin in the round and work as foll:

Rib rnd: (K1, p1) to last st, k1.

Rep rib rnd until cuff meas 13¾in (35cm).

Thumbhole rnd: Patt as set to last 3 sts, cast off 2 sts, k1.

Next rnd: Patt as set to cast-off sts, cast on 2 sts, k1.

Cont in rib until cuff meas 15¾in (40cm).

Cast off.

TO FINISH

Weave in ends and block according to yarn band instructions, taking care to open out the lace sections.

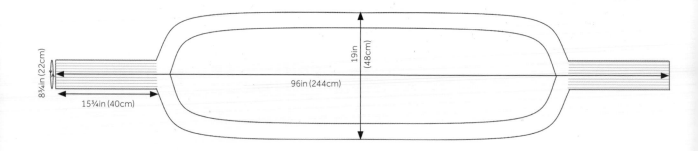

Golden shred

This glorious hand-dyed yarn is the colour of marmalade, and that shade inspired a lace rib pattern designed to look like orange segments. Wear a pair of funky sandals to show off these pretty socks, knitted from the top down with a heel flap, or cosy up at home and get yourself in the mood for breakfast.

SIZE
To fit: UK women's size 5-7
(US 7-9; Europe 37.5-40)
Ankle circumference: 6½in (16cm)
(stretchy)
Foot length: 10¼in (26cm) (adjustable)

YOU WILL NEED
Ginger's Hand Dyed Sheepish Sock
80% superwash British Bluefaced
Leicester, 20% nylon
(approx 400yd/365m per 100g)
1 x 100g hank in Melon Balls on Fire
2.5mm double-pointed or
    circular needles
Stitch markers
Tapestry needle

Note: Yarn amounts given are based
on average requirements and are
approximate.

TENSION
35 sts and 46 rnds to 10cm over patt
after blocking.
*Use larger or smaller needles if
necessary to obtain correct tension.*

TIP
Use a set of five dpns and divide the
pattern into four 15-st repeats.

NOTE ON ADJUSTING LENGTH
Each 15-st, 14-row patt rep meas
1½in (4cm) wide x 1¼in (3cm) long.
That means you can extend or shorten
the length of the foot or cuff by multiples
of 1¼in (3cm) by adding or subtracting
pattern repeats. To lengthen or shorten
the leg by a shorter amount simply add
rib rounds to the cuff.
To lengthen or shorten the foot by
a shorter amount work in st st after
your last patt rep before beginning
toe decreases.
Toe decreases are worked over
1¾in (4.5cm).

ORANGE SEGMENT LACE
Worked over 15 sts and 14 rnds
Rnd 1: K1, p2, yo, ssk, k2, sl1p, k2,
k2tog, yo, p2, k1.

ORANGE SEGMENT LACE

Rnd 2 and all alt rnds: K1, p2, k9, p2, k1.
Rnd 3: K1, p2, k1, yo, ssk, k1, sl1p, k1,
k2tog, yo, k1, p2, k1.
Rnd 5: K1, p2, k2, yo, ssk, sl1p, k2tog,
yo, k2, p2, k1.
Rnd 7: K1, p2, k2, yo, k2tog, sl1p, ssk,
yo, k2, p2, k1.
Rnd 9: K1, p2, k1, yo, k2tog, k1, sl1p, k1,
ssk, yo, k1, p2, k1.
Rnd 11: K1, p2, yo, k2tog, k2, sl1p, k2,
ssk, yo, p2, k1.
Rnd 13: K1, p2, k4, sl1p, k4, p2, k1.
Rnd 14: As rnd 2.

SOCK (MAKE 2)
Cast on 60 sts. Join to work in the
round, taking care not to twist sts,
and pm to mark beg of rnd.
Rib rnd: (K1, p1) around.

KEY

☐	knit
•	purl
V	sl1p
O	yo
/	k2tog
\	ssk

Rep rib rnd until piece meas approx ¾in (1.5cm).

Knit 1 rnd.

SET ORANGE SEGMENT LACE

Rnd 1: Work rnd 1 of Orange Segment Lace patt 4 times around.

Rnd 1 sets position of patt. Rep 14-rnd patt a total of 4 times in length.

HEEL FLAP

Rnd 1: K30, pm, turn and work on these 30 sts only for heel flap.

Row 1 (WS): (Sl1, p1) to end, turn.

Row 2: Sl1, k to end.

Rep these 2 rows 15 more times, ending with row 2. Heel flap meas approx 2½in (6.5cm).

TURN HEEL

Short row 1 (WS): Sl1, p15, p2tog, p1, turn.

Short row 2: Sl1, k3, ssk, k1, turn.

Short row 3: Sl1, p4 (to last st before gap), p2tog, p1, turn.

Short row 4: Sl1, k5 (to last st before gap), ssk, k1, turn.

Cont as set by rows 3 and 4 until no sts rem after gap, ending with a RS row. The last 2 rows will not have a k1 or p1 after the ssk or p2tog (16 sts).

REJOIN IN THE ROUND

After last row of heel turn, a RS row 4, do not turn but rejoin in the rnd as foll:
Pm (temporary beg of rnd marker), pick up and k1 st in each of 16 slipped sts up side of heel flap and 1 st in between heel flap and sts for top of foot, sm (original beg of rnd marker), patt across 30 sts for top of foot as set, pm, pick up and k1 st between top of foot and heel flap and 16 sts down side of heel flap, k across 16 heel sts (80 sts).

Set-up rnd: K13 tbl, (k2tog) twice, sm, patt to next m, sm, (ssk) twice, k13 tbl, k to end.

Next rnd: K to first top of foot marker, sm, patt to next m, sm, k to end.

Dec rnd: K to 2 sts before first top of foot marker, k2tog, sm, patt to next m, sm, ssk, k to end.

Rep last 2 rnds until 60 sts rem: 30 in patt for top of foot and 30 in st st across sole. Remove temporary beg of rnd marker. First top of foot marker now returns to being your beg of rnd marker and second top of foot marker shows halfway point.

FOOT

Cont straight as now set until a total of 9 patt reps have been worked from start of sock and sole meas approx 8½in (22cm) from tip of heel.

SECOND SOCK SYNDROME

Sock knitting is brilliant fun, but there's something about that second sock that just seems so much harder than the first. Here are a few tips and tricks to help:

- Cast on your second sock as soon as you finish the first.
- Knit lots of single socks, then knit the second one when you need it.
- Knit two socks at the same time using the magic loop method—find out how online.
- Reject peer pressure and wear mismatched socks. If someone asks you why your socks don't match, ask them why theirs do.

SET TOE DECREASES

Toe dec rnd: *K1, ssk, k to 3 sts before halfway m, k2tog, k1, sm; rep from * to end.

Knit 2 rnds.

Rep the last 3 rnds once more, then work toe dec rnd every alt rnd until 24 sts rem.

GRAFT TOE

Divide rem 24 sts over 2 needles: 12 sts on the front and 12 sts on the back needle, with the working yarn at the RH end.

Break yarn leaving a long tail and graft toe sts tog using Kitchener stitch.

TO FINISH

Weave in ends.

Block to open out lace pattern.

Shadow and light

'I would know my shadow and my light, so shall I at last be whole,' runs the final chorus of Sir Michael Tippett's secular oratorio *A Child of Our Time*. This jumper, knitted in the round from the top down, has a dark side and a light side as it's completely reversible. Embrace every part of yourself as you enjoy the gentle rhythm of brioche knitting and quick progress in super-soft, chunky yarn.

SIZES

S[M:L]

Actual bust: 57½[64:70]in (146[162:178]cm)

Length: 22in (56cm) (adjustable)

Sleeve length: 8½in (21.5cm) (adjustable)

Figures in square brackets refer to larger sizes: where there is only one set of figures this refers to all sizes.

YOU WILL NEED

Cascade Aereo Tweed 38% Merino wool, 25% baby alpaca, 22% nylon, 10% acrylic, 5% viscose (approx 240yd/220m per 100g)

3[3:3] x 100g balls in 306 (A)

3[3:3] x 100g balls in 304 (B)

5mm and 5.5mm circular needles

Spare 5.5mm circular needle

Cable needle

Stitch markers

Stitch holders or scrap yarn

Note: Yarn amounts given are based on average requirements and are approximate.

PATTERN NOTES

This garment is created with a large amount of positive ease – check how much ease you want and knit the size that best suits you. The sample is size 2 and is worn by Caitlin, a UK size 6-8, on page 59 and by Caprice-Kwai, who is size 6-8 on top and 10-12 on the hips, on page 60. The short-row shaping to create a flattering scoop at the back hem is quite tricky and is optional. The garment is completely reversible, but is described in the pattern instructions as having a RS and WS, with colour A dominant on the RS.

TENSION

10 sts and 18 rnds to 4in (10cm) over two-colour brioche using 5.5mm needles.

Use larger or smaller needles if necessary to obtain correct tension.

YOKE

Using 5mm needles and A, cast on 62 sts using long-tail cast on. Join to work in the round, taking care not to twist sts, and pm to mark beg of rnd.

Set-up rnd 1: Using A, (k1, sl1yo) around.

Set-up rnd 2: Using B, (sl1yo, brp1) around.

Rnd 1: Using A, (brk1, sl1yo) around.

Rnd 2: Using B, (sl1yo, brp1) around.

Rep rnds 1 and 2 seven more times.

SET INCREASE AND CABLE PATT

Change to 5.5mm needles.

Set-up rnd 1: Using A, brk1, sl1yo, pm1, (brk1, sl1yo) 9 times, pm for cable, (brk1, sl1yo) 5 times, pm2, (brk1, sl1yo) twice, pm3, (brk1, sl1yo) 13 times, pm4, brk1, sl1yo.

Set-up rnd 2: Using B, (sl1yo, brp1) around, slipping markers.

Rnd 1: Using A, (brk1, sl1yo) to m1, sm, br4stinc, sl1yo, (brk1, sl1yo) to cable marker, sm, C8Br, *(brk1, sl1yo) to m, sm, br4stinc, sl1yo; rep from * 2 more times, (brk1, sl1yo) to end (inc 16).

Rnd 2: Using B, *(sl1yo, brp1) to m, remove m, sl1yo, p1, pm, sl1yo, p1; rep from * 3 more times, sl1yo, (brp1, sl1yo) to end.

Rnd 3: Using A, (brk1, sl1yo) around.

Rnd 4: Using B, (sl1yo, brp1) around.

Rnds 5-8: As rnds 3 and 4.

Rnd 9: Using A, *(brk1, sl1yo) to m, sm, br4stinc, sl1yo; rep from * 3 more times, (brk1, sl1yo) to end (inc 16).

Rnd 10: As rnd 2.

Rnds 11-16: As rnds 3 and 4.

These 16 rnds set cable and raglan patt, inc 32 sts over each full patt rep. Rep rnds 1-16 a further 4[5:6] times, ending with rnd 16.

222[254:286] sts.

SPLIT FOR BODY AND SLEEVES

Next rnd: Using A, (brk1, sl1yo) to m1, remove m and slip 22[26:30] sts just

worked to holder for Right Sleeve, (brk1, sl1yo) to cable marker, sm, C8Br, (brk1, sl1yo) to next m, remove m, brk1, sl1yo, pm, (brk1, sl1yo) to m3, slip 42[50:58] sts just worked to holder for Left Sleeve, **cast on 13 sts to LH needle using knitted method, slip last front st to LH needle, pass cast-on st over last front st, slip front st back to RH needle**, pm at centre of cast-on sts to mark halfway point, (k1, sl1yo) 3 times, pm, (k1, sl1yo) 3 times, (brk1, sl1yo) to m4, remove marker, brk1, sl1yo, pm, (brk1, sl1yo) to end, slip 20[24:28] sts just worked to holder for Right Sleeve, break A and B, rejoin A and rep from ** to **, (k1, sl1yo) 6 times, slip 6 sts back to LH needle, pm to mark new beg of rnd. 162[178:194] sts for Body: 82[90:98] for front and 80[88:96] for back. 42[50:58] sts on each holder for Sleeves.

BODY

Rnd 1: Using B, (sl1yo, brp1) around.
Rnd 2: Using A, (brk1, sl1yo) around.
Rnd 3: Using B, (sl1yo, brp1) around.
Rnds 4-15: As rnds 3 and 4.
Rnd 16: Using A, (brk1, sl1yo) to cable m, sm, C8Br, (brk1, sl1yo) to end.
Rep these 16 rows until you have worked 10 full patt reps or until you reach desired length, ending on rnd 16. Then work rnds 1-5 again.

SHAPE BACK HEM (OPTIONAL)

Note: For a straight back hem, skip this section and cont from *** for cast off.
Short row 1 (RS): Using A, (brk1, sl1yo) across front to halfway point marker, sm, brk1, sl1yo, change to spare 5.5mm circular needle, (brk1, sl1yo) to last 4 sts, yf, slip next st and its yo to RH needle, yb, slip 3 rem sts of rnd to RH needle.
Short row 2 (RS): Using B and main 5.5mm needle, (sl1yo, brp1) from start of rnd to start of spare needle and then across spare needle to wrapped st, wyif slip wrapped st to RH (main) needle, yb,

slip rem 3 unworked sts to end of rnd on to the RH needle so they sit next to beg of rnd marker. All sts are now on main needle. From this point the short rows will be worked on the spare needle and the main needle holds all those sts not being worked.

Short row 3 (WS): Using A and spare needle, (sl1yo, brp1) to 5 sts before halfway marker, sl1yo, yf, slip next st and its yo to RH needle, yb, slide sts on spare needle back to other end to work this side again.

Short row 4 (WS): Using B and the other tip of spare needle, (brk1, sl1yo) to st before wrapped st, brk1, yf, slip wrapped st to RH needle, take yarn to back, slip wrapped st back to main needle, turn.

Short row 5 (RS): Using A and spare needle, (sl1yo, brk1) to last 4 sts on spare needle, yf, slip st and its yo to RH needle, yb and slip rem 3 unworked sts to main needle. Do not turn, slide sts to other end of needle to work this side again.

Short row 6 (RS): Using B and spare needle, (brp1, sl1yo) to 1 st before wrapped st, brp1, yf, slip next st, yb, slip st to main needle, turn.

Short rows 7-10: As short rows 3-6.

Short rows 11 and 12: As short rows 3 and 4.

Next row (RS): Using A and spare needle tip, patt to end of spare needle, then patt to end of rnd, brioche-knitting wraps tog with sts and their yarn overs as you come to them.

Next rnd: Patt in B.
Change to 5mm needle.

Rep rnds 2 and 3 of main body patt 4 times.

***Using A, cast off very loosely as foll: Brk1, *p1, pass first st on RH needle over second st, brk1, pass first st on RH needle over second st; rep from * to last st, p1, pass first st on RH needle over second st, fasten off.

LEFT SLEEVE

Slip 42[50:58] sts from Left Sleeve holder to 5.5mm needle.

Using A, pick up and k16 sts across underarm, one in each st. 58[66:74] sts. Break A and slip 8 sts to LH needle, pm for beg of rnd.**

Next rnd: Using B, (sl1yo, p1) 4 times, (sl1yo, brp1) 10 times, pm, (sl1yo, brp1) to last 8 sts, (sl1yo, p1) to end.

***Rnd 1:** Using A, (brk1, sl1yo) to m, sm, C8Br, (brk1, sl1yo) to end.

Rnd 2: Using B, (sl1yo, brp1) around.

Rnd 3: Using A, (brk1, sl1yo) around.

Rnd 4: Using B, (sl1yo, brp1) around.

Rep rnds 3 and 4 five more times.

Rep rnds 1-4 once more.

Change to 5mm needles.

Rep rnds 3 and 4 another 22 times.

Using A, cast off loosely as for Body.

RIGHT SLEEVE

Work as for Left Sleeve to **.

Next rnd: Using B, (sl1yo, p1) 4 times, (sl1yo, brp1) 11 times, pm, (sl1yo, brp1) to last 8 sts, (sl1yo, p1) to end.

Work as Left Sleeve from *** to end.

TO FINISH

Weave in ends very neatly using duplicate stitch so jumper can be fully reversible. Fold over Sleeve ends and if necessary stitch in place.

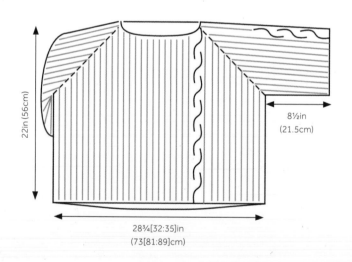

22in (56cm)

8½in (21.5cm)

28¾[32:35]in (73[81:89]cm)

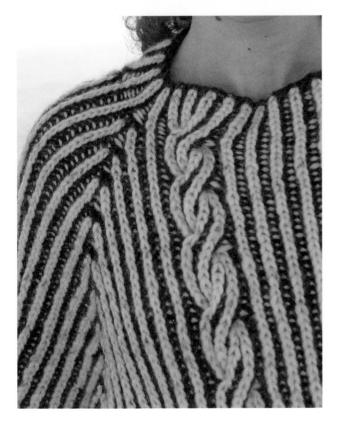

Force field

My children Stanley and Daisy are moving into the tween to teenage years and growing more and more independent. As I send them out to explore the world on their own, I wish I could set up a force field around them to keep them safe and feeling loved out there in the great wide open. Warm, fluffy alpaca thread held together with soft Merino wool adds extra warmth but no weight to this cosy cardigan, and the pretty Japanese stitch pattern on the pockets is a sign that the wearer is wrapped up in the love of his or her knitter.

SIZES
To fit age: 4-6[6-8:8-10:10-12] yrs
To fit chest: 24[25½:29:31½]in (61[65:74:80]cm)
Length to underarm: 8¾[9½:10¼:11]in (22[24:26:28]cm)
Width at chest: 14¾[17¾:19¾:21¾]in (37.5[45:50:55]cm)
Length to shoulder: 13½[15:16½:18]in (34[38:42:46]cm)
Sleeve length: 13½[15¼:18:19¾]in (34[39:46:50]cm)
Pocket width: 6in (15cm)
Pocket length: 4¼in (11cm)
Figures in square brackets refer to larger sizes: where there is only one set of figures this applies to all sizes.

YOU WILL NEED
Lang Yarns Merino 150 100% Merino wool (approx 164yd/150m per 50g) 4[5:5:6] x 50g balls in shade 0119 (A)
Lang Yarns Alpaca Superlight 54% alpaca, 24% nylon, 22% wool (approx 218yd/199m per 25g) 3[4:4:4] x 25g balls in shade 0065 (B)
5.5mm and 4mm circular needles
5.5mm double-pointed needles (optional)
Stitch holders
Stitch markers
Cable needle

4mm crochet hook
4 x 1in (28mm) diameter buttons

Note: Yarn amounts given are based on average requirements and are approximate.

TENSION
16 sts and 23 rows to 4in (10cm) over st st using 5.5mm needle with one strand each of A and B held together. 23 sts and 27 rows to 4in (10cm) over st st using 4mm needle and A only. *Use larger or smaller needles if necessary to obtain correct tension.*

PATTERN NOTES
Size 3 is photographed on Daisy, who is a tall nine-year-old.

BUTTONHOLES
Only the first buttonhole, on row 7, is referred to in the pattern. Work buttonholes on the following rows:
Size 1: 7, 23, 37, 53
Size 2: 7, 23, 29, 55
Size 3: 7, 25, 41, 59
Size 4: 7, 27, 45, 65

POCKET PATTERN
Worked over 25 sts and 16 rows
Row 1 (RS): *P1, (k1 tbl, p1) twice*, (k2tog, k1, yo, k1) twice, yo, k1, ssk, k1,
yo, k1, ssk; rep from * to * once more.
Row 2: PK1, (p1 tbl, k1) twice, p15, (k1, p1 tbl) twice, PK1.
Row 3: *(P1, k1 tbl) twice, p1*, yo, ssk, k1, k2tog, k1, yo, k3, yo, k1, ssk, k1, k2tog, yo; rep from * to * once more.
Rows 4, 6 and 8: PK1, (p1 tbl, k1) twice, k1, p13, k1, (k1, p1 tbl) twice, PK1.
Row 5: P1, TW3, p2, yo, k3tog, k1, yo, k2, MB, k2, yo, k1, sssk, yo, p2, TW3, p1.
Row 7: (P1, k1 tbl) twice, p2, k2tog, k1, yo, k7, yo, k1, ssk, p2, (k1 tbl, p1) twice.
Row 9: As row 1.
Row 10: As row 2.
Row 11: As row 3.
Rows 12 and 14: As row 4.
Row 13: P1, TW3, p2, yo, k3tog, k1, yo, k5, yo, k1, sssk, yo, p2, TW3, p1.
Row 15: As row 7.
Row 16: As row 4.

BODY
Cast on 131[155:171:187] sts.
Broken rib row 1: (K1, p1) to last st, k1.
Broken rib row 2: Purl.
Rep these 2 rows 2 more times.
Buttonhole row: (K1, p1) twice, cast off 2 sts (1 st left on needle), (p1, k1) to end.
Next row: P to gap, cast on 2 sts over cast-off sts, p to end.
Rep broken rib rows 1 and 2 twice more, then work row 1 again.

Next row (WS – dec): P65[77:85:93], p2tog, p to end. 130[154:170:186] sts. Rib meas 2in (5cm).

SET BODY PATT

Row 1 (RS): (K1, p1) 5 times, k25[31:35:39], pm, k60[72:80:88], pm, k25[31:35:39], (p1, k1) to end.

Row 2: Purl, slipping markers.

These 2 rows set main Body patt with 130[154:170:184] sts: 60[72:80:88] for back, 35[41:45:49] for each front and 10 sts in broken rib at each edge.

Rep rows 1 and 2 once more, slipping markers.

SET POCKETS

Row 1 (RS): (K1, p1) 5 times, *k0[3:5:7], pm, (k1, yo) 24 times, k1, pm*, k to end of back section slipping markers, sm; rep from * to *, k0[3:5:7], (p1, k1) 5 times.

Row 2: P to first pocket marker, sm, p across pocket sts slipping all yarn overs on to a holder, sm, p to next pocket marker, p across pocket sts slipping all yarn overs on to a separate 4mm circular needle, p to end.

POCKET LINING (MAKE 2)

You now have 24 sts on a 4mm needle. With RS of main piece facing and a new ball of A only, work as foll:

**Row 1 (RS – inc): K2, (kfb, k1) 10 times, k2 (34 sts).

Row 2: Purl.

Row 3: Sl1, k to end.

Row 4: Sl1, p to end.

Rep rows 3 and 4 another 13 times.**

Slip these sts on to a holder, slip 24 sts held for other pocket lining to 4mm circular needle, then using the same separate ball of A only, work from ** to ** once more.

Pocket linings meas 4¼in (11cm).

SET SEAMLESS POCKETS

Return to main piece and, using 5.5mm needles and 1 strand each of A and B held together, work as foll:

Set-up row 1 (RS): (K1, p1) 5 times, k to 1 st before pocket marker,*PK1, sm, (p1, k1) twice, p2, k13, p2, (k1, p1) twice, sm, PK1*, k to 1 st before next pocket marker; rep from * to *, k to last 10 sts, (p1, k1) 5 times.

Set-up row 2: P to pocket marker, *sm, p1, k1, p1, k2, p13, k2, p1, k1, p1, sm*, p to next pocket marker; rep from * to * once more, p to end.

Row 1: (K1, p1) 5 times, k to pocket marker, *sm, work row 1 of Pocket Patt, sm*, k to next pocket marker; rep from * to *, k to last 10 sts, (p1, k1) 5 times.

Row 2: P to pocket marker, *sm, work row 2 of Pocket Patt, sm*, p to next pocket marker; rep from * to *, p to end.

These 2 rows set Pocket Patt.

Cont in patt as set until you have worked all 16 rows of patt, then work rows 1-8 once more.

END POCKETS

Next row (RS): (K1, p1) 5 times, *k to pocket marker, remove marker, slip pocket sts to holder then work on lining sts as foll: k4, (k2tog, k1) 8 times, k2tog, k4, remove pocket m; rep from * once more, k to last 10 sts, (p1, k1) 5 times. 130[154:170:184] sts: 60[72:80:88] for back and 35[41:45:49] for each front.

Next row: Purl.

Now cont in Body patt for 10[12:16:22] more rows.

Body meas approx 8¾[9½:10:11]in (22[24:25:28]cm)

Set aside.

LEFT SLEEVE

With 5.5mm circular or double-pointed needles and 1 strand each of A and B held tog, cast on 26[26:30:30] sts.

Join to work in the rnd, taking care not to twist sts, and pm for beg of rnd.

Broken rib rnd 1: (K1, p1) around.

Broken rib rnd 2: Knit.

Rep rnds 1 and 2 a further 7[8:9:9] times. Piece meas 2[2¼:2¾:2¾]in (5[6:7:7]cm).**

Thumbhole row: (K1, p1) twice, cast off 4 sts (1 st left on needle), (p1, k1) to end.

***Next row: K to gap, cast on 4 sts over cast-off sts, k to end.

Cont in broken rib for 8[12:16:16] more rnds until rib meas 4[4¼:5½:5½]in (10[11:14:14]cm), ending with rnd 2.

SET MAIN PATT AND INCS

Next rnd: Knit.

Next rnd (inc): K1, m1L, k to last st, m1R, k1 (inc 2).

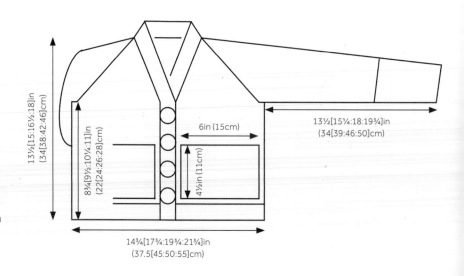

Knit 3 rnds.

Rep last 4 rnds 6[10:11:13] more times. 40[48:54:58] sts.

Cont straight in st st until Sleeve meas 9½[11:12½:14¼]in (24[28:32:36]cm) from end of ribbed cuff.

Slip 5[6:6:7] sts on each side of beg of rnd marker to a holder – 10[12:12:14] sts on hold for underarm.

Set aside.

RIGHT SLEEVE

Work as Left Sleeve to **.

Thumbhole row: (K1, p1) to last 8 sts, cast off 4 sts (1 st left on needle), (p1, k1) to end.

Work as Left Sleeve to end.

YOKE

JOIN BODY AND SLEEVES

With RS facing, 5.5mm needles and 1 strand each of A and B held tog, beg at edge of Body sts, work as foll:

Set-up row: (K1, p1) 5 times, k20[25:29:32] (right front), pm, slip next 10[12:12:14] sts on to a holder for underarm, k across 30[36:42:44] sts for right Sleeve, pm, k50[60:68:74] for back, pm, slip next 10[12:12:14] sts on to a holder for underarm, k across 30[36:42:44] sts for left Sleeve, pm, k20[25:29:32], (p1, k1) 5 times (left front). 170[202:230:246] sts: 50[60:68:74] for back, 30[35:39:42] for each front and 30[36:42:44] for each Sleeve.

Next row: Purl.

SET RAGLAN DECREASES

Row 1 (RS): (K1, p1) 5 times, ssk, *k to

3 sts before m, k2tog, k1, sm, k1, ssk; rep from * 3 more times, k to last 12 sts, k2tog, (p1, k1) 5 times (dec 10). 160[192:220:236] sts.

Row 2: Purl.

Row 3: (K1, p1) 5 times, *k to 3 sts before m, k2tog, k1, sm, k1, ssk; rep from * 3 more times, k to last 10 sts, (p1, k1) 5 times (dec 8). 152[184:212:228] sts.

Row 4: Purl.

Rep last 4 rows 5[7:8:9] more times. 62[58:68:66] sts: 26[28:32:34] sts for back, 12[11:12:12] sts each front and 6[4:6:4] sts for each Sleeve.

SIZES 1, 3 AND 4 ONLY

Next row (RS): (K1, p1) 4 times, k1, sssp, sm, *k1[-:1:0], ssk, k2tog, k1[-:1:0]*, sm, k1, ssk, k to 3 sts before m, k2tog, k1, sm; rep from * to * once more, sm, p3tog, k1, (p1, k1) to end.

SIZE 2 ONLY

Next row (RS): (K1, p1) 4 times, k1, ssp, sm, *ssk, k2tog*, sm, k1, ssk, k to 3 sts before m, k2tog, k1, sm; rep from * to * once more, sm, p2tog, k1, (p1, k1) to end.

ALL SIZES

52[50:58:56] sts rem: 24[26:30:32] for back, 10 for each front and 4[2:4:2] for each Sleeve.

Next row: Purl.

NECKBAND

Pm at centre of back sts (after 12[13:15:16] sts).

Next row (RS): (K1, p1) 4 times, k1, p2tog (last rib band st with first Sleeve st), turn.

Next row: Sl1, p to end.

Rep last 2 rows across 2[1:3:1] rem Sleeve sts and 12[13:15:16] sts for first half of back. Put rem 10 sts on hold and break yarn.

With WS facing, rejoin yarn to rib sts at other edge.

Next row (WS): (P1, k1) 4 times, p1, ssk (last rib band st with first Sleeve st), turn.

Next row (RS): Sl1 wyib, k to end.

Work as for first side until all Sleeve and back sts have been worked and you have reached the held sts for first band.

Return held sts to needle and graft together using Kitchener stitch.

TO FINISH

Graft underarms using Kitchener stitch.

POCKET TOPS (MAKE 2)

With RS facing, slip 25 held sts for pocket back to 5.5mm needle.

With 1 strand each of A and B held tog, work as foll:

Row 1 (RS – dec): PP1, k1, p1, k1, p2tog, k2tog, (p1, k1) 4 times, p1, ssk, p2tog tbl, k1, p1, k1, PP1 (21 sts).

Row 2: Purl.

Row 3: PP1, (k1, p1) to last 2 sts, k1, PP1.

Row 4: Purl.

Rep row 3 once more, then cast off pwise on WS.

Sew on buttons to match buttonholes.

Weave in ends.

Block, pinning out pockets to open lace patt.

Blanketed in love

Patchwork blankets are a delight to look at, but I'd never want to do that much sewing. Knitting mitred squares is a simple and effective way to get that great blocky patchwork look without ending up with hundreds of little squares to sew together. And it's wonderfully cosy, to wrap you up and blanket you in love as you knit.

SIZE
Width: 47¼in (120cm)
Length: 66in (168cm)
Each square meas: 9½in (24cm) square

YOU WILL NEED
Cascade Yarns Magnum
100% Peruvian Highland wool
(approx 123yd/112.5m per 250g)
4 x 250g hanks in 9478 Cotton Candy (A)
6 x 250g hanks in 9431 Regal Red (B)
12mm needles
Stitch markers

Note: Yarn amounts given are based on average requirements and are approximate.

HEART SQUARE 1
Using A, cast on 17 sts.
Knit 3 rows.
Next row (WS): K2, p to last 2 sts, k2.
SET CHART
Next row: K2, p row 1 of Heart Chart, k2.
Next row: K2, k row 2 of Heart Chart, k2.
These 2 rows set position of
Heart Chart.
Cont as set until all 19 rows of Heart Chart are complete.
Next row (WS): K2, p to last 3 sts, k2.
Next row: Knit.
Knit 2 rows.
Cast off.

GARTER STITCH SQUARE 1
Worked on row 1 only
Pick up 18 sts down left edge of previous square, then cast on 17 sts using a cable or knitted cast on (35 sts).
**Set-up row (WS): K17, pm, k to end.
SET G ST PATT
Row 1 (RS): K to 2 sts before m, remove m, sk2po, pm, k to end (dec 2).
Row 2: K to m, sm, p1, k to end.
Rep rows 1 and 2 until 3 sts rem.
Next row: Sk2po.
Fasten off.

GARTER STITCH SQUARE 2
Worked at starting edge of rows 2-7
Using a long tail cast on, cast on 17 sts, then pick up 18 sts along top edge of square on row below.
Work as Garter Stitch Square row 1 from ** to end.

GARTER STITCH SQUARE 3
Worked in all other positions on rows 2-7
Pick up 18 sts down left edge of previous square and 17 sts across top edge of square on row below.
Work as Garter Stitch Square row 1 from ** to end.

STRIPY SQUARE
Using A, pick up 17 sts down left edge of previous square and 16 sts across

top edge of square on row below.
Set-up row (WS): P16, pm, p to end.
Change to B.
Row 1 (RS): K to 2 sts before m, remove m, sk2po, pm, k to end.
Row 2: P to end, slipping marker.
Change to A.
Rows 3 and 4: As rows 1 and 2.

HEART CHART

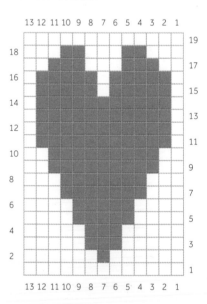

KEY
☐ RS: knit, WS: purl
■ B
☐ A

Cont in st st and, keeping stripe patt correct, rep rows 1-4 until 3 sts rem.
Next row: Sk2po.
Fasten off.

HEART SQUARE 2

Using A, pick up and k14 sts down side of last square and 17 sts across top of square on row below (31 sts).
Next row (WS): K16, k2tog, turn (30 sts).
Next row: K to end.
Next row: K2, p13, k1, k2tog, turn (29 sts).

SET HEART CHART
Next row (RS): K2, k row 1 of Heart Chart, k2.
Next row: K2, p row 2 of Heart Chart, k1, k2tog, turn.
These 2 rows set position of Heart Chart. Cont as set until all 19 rows of Heart Chart are complete, then cont in A only (20 sts).
Next row (WS): K2, p13, k1, k2tog (19 sts).
Next row: Knit.
Next row (WS): K16, k2tog, turn (18 sts).
Next row: K2tog, cast off all rem sts.

BLANKET CONSTRUCTION

Work squares in number order, starting with Square 1 and working through to Square 35. At the end of Square 35 the blanket will be complete.

SQUARE 1
Work Heart Square 1.

SQUARES 2 AND 4
Using B, work Garter Stitch Square 1.

SQUARES 3 AND 5
Using A, work Garter Stitch Square 1.

SQUARES 6, 16 AND 26
Using B, work Garter Stitch Square 2.

SQUARES 11, 21 AND 31
Using A, work Garter Stitch Square 2.

SQUARES 7, 9, 17, 19, 27 AND 29
Work Stripy Square.

SQUARES 8, 10, 12, 14, 18, 20, 22, 24, 28, 30, 32 AND 34
Using B, work Garter Stitch Square 3.

SQUARES 13, 15, 23, 25 AND 33
Using A, work Garter Stitch Square 3.

SQUARE 35
Work Heart Square 2.

TO FINISH
Weave in ends.

35 ♥	34	33	32	31
30	29	28	27	26
25	24	23	22	21
20	19	18	17	16
15	14	13	12	11
10	9	8	7	6
5	4	3	2	1 ♥

Get involved

Now you've got the hang of it, get your teeth
into some unusually constructed designs.

Happy day

Picture a day that's sparkling with frost or thick, deep snow in bright winter sunshine. These cosy Fairisle mittens will keep your fingers toasty while you enjoy the great outdoors thanks to the alpaca and wool yarn and the stranded colourwork, which gives you an extra layer of cosiness, perfect for a happy day!

SIZE
Cuff circumference: 4½in (12cm)
Hand circumference: 6¼in (16cm)
Length: 6¼in (16cm)

YOU WILL NEED
Manos del Uruguay Alpaca Heather
70% wool, 30% alpaca
(approx 164yd/150m per 50g)
1 x 50g hank in Toast Undyed (A)
1 x 50g hank in Honeycomb (B)
1 x 50g hank in Cinnamon (C)
Small amount of smooth scrap yarn
3.25mm and 4mm circular
    or double-pointed needles
Stitch markers

Note: Yarn amounts given are based on average requirements and are approximate.

TENSION
25 sts and 25 rows to 4in (10cm) over colourwork patt using 4mm needles. *Use larger or smaller needles if necessary to obtain correct tension.*

RIGHT MITTEN
Using 3.25mm needles and C cast on 40 sts. Join to work in the round, taking care not to twist sts, and pm to mark beg of rnd and after 20 sts for halfway point.
Change to A.
Rib rnd: (K1, p1) around.
Rep rib rnd until Mitten meas 2¼in (6cm).

SET COLOURWORK PATT
Change to 4mm needles.
Starting with rnd 1, work in patt from Chart twice around, stranding yarn not in use across back of work.
On rnd 25 set afterthought thumb as foll:
Next rnd: Patt 2, work next 6 sts using scrap yarn. Slip sts just worked back to LH needle and work again using main yarn, patt to end.

CHART

KEY

☐	knit
☐	A
▨	B
■	C
◺	ssk
◹	k2tog
☐	Right Mitten thumbhole
☐	Left Mitten thumbhole
☒	no stitch

Cont in patt until you have worked rnd 45 of Chart.

SET DECREASES

Cont working in colour patt from Chart and dec as foll:

Next rnd: *Ssk, patt to last 2 sts before halfway point marker, k2tog; rep from * once more (dec 4).

Rep last rnd until 4 sts rem (rnd 55 of Chart).

Break yarn, pull through rem sts and pull tight to fasten off.

THUMB

Using A and 3.25mm needles, pick up 6 sts across bottom of scrap yarn sts, 1 st in space between bottom and top sts, 6 sts across top and 1 st in between top and bottom (14 sts).

Knit 18 rnds.

SET DECREASES

Next rnd: (K1, k2tog) to last 2 sts, k2 (10 sts).

Next rnd: (K2tog) around (5 sts).

Break yarn, pull through rem sts and pull tight to fasten off.

LEFT MITTEN

Work as Right Mitten, but on rnd 25 of Chart set afterthought thumb as foll:

Rnd 25: Patt 12, work next 6 sts in scrap yarn, slip these 6 sts back to LH needle and work again using main yarn, patt to end.

Now cont as for Right Mitten to end.

TO FINISH

Weave in ends.

Wrap in a wet tea towel and press under a hot iron.

Lilies of the field

Knitting can help you to escape from your worries in so many ways: the rhythmic motion of stitching calms troubled spirits; the feeling of soft yarn passing through your fingers is deeply soothing; and learning new skills can be so absorbing that the sheer act of concentration can lift you out of any anxiety, discomfort or tribulation you may be experiencing. This camisole features intriguing techniques which I hope will offer you some beautiful calm moments, as peaceful as the lilies of the field.

SIZES

To fit: 30[32:34:36:38:40:42:44]in (76[81:86:91:97:102:107:112]cm)

Actual bust: 29[29½:31:33½:36¼:37¾:39¼:42½]in (73[75:79:85:92:96:100:108]cm)

Hem circumference: 30¾[33:35¾:37½:42:45:47¼:51½]in (78[84:91:95:107:114:120:131]cm)

Waist circumference: 26¾[27½: 28¾:30¼:34¼:35½:37:40¼]in (68[70:73:77:87:90:94:102]cm)

Length to shoulder: 23in (58cm)

Figures in square brackets refer to larger sizes: where there is only one set of figures this applies to all sizes.

YOU WILL NEED

McIntosh Calm 80% extra fine Merino wool, 20% cashmere (approx 150m per 50g)
3[3:4:4:5:6:7:8] x 50g cake in Dragonfruit (A)
1 x 50g cakes in Raspberry (B)
3 x 4mm circular needles 80cm long
Stitch holders
Stitch markers

Note: Yarn amounts given are based on average requirements and are approximate.

TENSION

21 sts and 32 rows to 4in (10cm) over st st.
Lace panel meas 6in (15cm) wide and 2¾in (7cm) long
Use smaller or larger needles if necessary to obtain correct tension.

PATTERN NOTE

Our model wears size 1 and is a UK 6-8.

LILIES OF THE FIELD

Worked over 32 sts and 24 rnds

Rnd 1: P1, k2, yo, ssk, p2, yo, k4, ssk, k6, k2tog, k4, yo, p2, k2, yo, ssk, p1.

Rnd 2: P1, k2tog, yo, k2, p2, k1, yo, k4, ssk, k4, k2tog, k4, yo, k1, p2, k2tog, yo, k2, p1.

Rnd 3: P1, k2, yo, ssk, p2, k2, yo, k4, ssk, k2, k2tog, k4, yo, k2, p2, k2, yo, ssk, p1.

Rnd 4: P1, k2tog, yo, k2, p2, k3, yo, k4, ssk, k2tog, k4, yo, k3, p2, k2tog, yo, k2, p1.

Rnds 5-12: Rep rnds 1-4 two more times.

Rnd 13: P1, k2, yo, ssk, p5, (k2, yo, ssk) 3 times, p5, k2, yo, ssk, p1.

Rnd 14: P1, k2tog, yo, k2, p5, (k2tog, yo, k2) 3 times, p5, k2tog, yo, k2, p1.

Rnds 15-24: Rep rnds 13 and 14 five more times.

These 24 rnds form pattern and are repeated.

FRONT HEM

Using 4mm needle and A, cast on 85[91:101:103:115:123:131:141] sts.

Row 1 (RS): (K1, yo) to last st, k1. 169[181:201:205:229:245:161:281] sts.

Next row: (P1, slip next st on to a second 4mm needle) to last st, p1. You now have 85[91:101:103:115:123:131:141] sts on first needle and 84[90:100:102:114:122:130:140] sts on second needle.

With original needle still attached and WS facing, join B to second needle and work across sts on second needle only as foll:

Row 1: (K1 tbl) to end.

Row 2: Sl1, p to end.

Row 3: Sl1, k to end.

Rep rows 2 and 3 once more, then row 2 again.

Set aside and return to first needle, using A and with RS facing.

Next row (RS): Insert RH needle tip into first st on LH needle, then use the same tip to pick up the first st in the first row of B section and k these 2 sts tog, k to end.

Next row: Insert RH needle tip into first st on LH needle, then use the same tip to pick up the first st of the second row of B section and p these 2 sts tog, p to end.

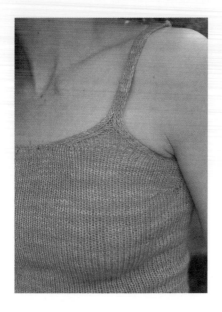

Rep last 2 rows 2 more times until A section matches B section, with edge sts knitted together and ending with a WS row.**

Next row: With RS of A section facing and using A, join the two sections by knitting together 1 st on first needle with 1 st on second needle until you are left with 1 st on first needle, k1. 85[91:101:103:115:123:131:141] sts.

BACK HEM

Work as front hem to **.

Next row: With RS of A section facing and using A, ktog 25[28:33: 34:40:44:48:53] sts from first and second needles, slip next 34 sts in B to a holder, working on the A sts only (k10, k2tog) twice, k10, then k tog the rem 26[29:34:35:41:45:49:54] sts from first and second needles. 83[89:99:101:113:121:129:139] sts in A remain on first needle and 34 sts in B on holder. Do not break yarn.

BACK PANEL

Slip A sts to a holder and return B sts to needle.

Working across these 34 sts with RS of A section facing (so with smooth side of st st facing the opposite way from the hem section) work as foll:

Row 1 (RS): Sl1, k to end.
Row 2: Sl1, p to end.
Rep these 2 rows until Panel meas 15¼in (39cm).
Slip sts to a holder.

BODY

Set-up row: Using A and with RS facing, starting with last st of Front Hem, pm, slip this st to needle holding Back Hem sts and k tog with first st of Back Hem, k23[26:30:32:38:42:45:51], pm, k next st tog with first edge st of Back Panel as on Hems, work rnd 1 of Lilies of the Field patt over next 32 sts, pm, k to last st of Back Hem, slip last st on to needle holding Front Hem and k tog with first st of Front Hem, pm to mark division between back and front, k to end. 166[178:198:202:226:242:258:278] sts: 84[90:100:102:114:122:130:140] sts for front and 82[88:98:100:112:120:128:138] sts for back.

The pieces are now joined together at both sides and you will work in the round from this point.

Rnd 1: Patt to m, sm, (this takes you to Lilies of the Field patt), k next st tog with second edge st of Back Panel, work rnd 2 of Lilies of the Field patt over next 32 sts, k next st tog with edge st of Back Panel, sm, k to end slipping markers.

Rnd 2: Patt to m, sm, work rnd 3 of Lilies of the Field patt to last st before m, k1, sm, k to end.

These 2 rnds set Lilies of the Field patt at back, with 1 st at each edge of patt worked together with a picked-up st from Back Panel to secure Back Panel to reverse of lace pattern on every alt rnd, and st st across the front.

SET WAIST SHAPING DECREASES

Cont in patt as set, working edge sts of Back Panel tog with sts on either side of Panel on every alt rnd, and shape waist as foll:

Next rnd (dec): K5, pm, ssk, patt as set to last 7 sts of back, k2tog, pm, k5, sm, k5, pm, ssk, k to last 7 sts of front, k2tog, pm, k to end. 162[174:194:198:222:238:254:274] sts.

KEY

☐	knit
•	purl
O	yo
\	ssk
/	k2tog
☐	Repeat 1
☐	Repeat 2

Patt as set for 9[6:5:5:4:3:3:2] rnds.

Next rnd (dec): K to dec marker, sm, ssk, k to 2 sts before next dec marker, k2tog, sm, k to next dec marker, sm, ssk, patt to 2 sts before next dec marker, k2tog, sm, k to end.

Rep last 10[7:6:6:5:4:4:3] rnds 4[6:9:8:9:11:13:14] more times.

142[146:154:162:182:190:198:214] sts.

Work 3 rnds straight in patt.

This should take you to rnd 8 of Lilies of the Field patt.

SET WAIST SHAPING INCREASES

Note: Dec markers will remain where they are but will now be referred to as inc markers and mark increase points.

Next rnd (inc): K to inc marker, sm, m1L, k to next inc marker, m1R, sm, k to next inc marker, sm, m1L, patt to next inc marker, m1R, sm, k to end.

146[150:158:166:186:194:202:218] sts.

Patt 15 rnds straight.

Rep inc rnd.

150[154:162:170:190:198:206:222] sts.

Rep last 16 rnds once more.

154[158:166:174:194:202:210:226] sts.

SIZE 4 ONLY

Rep last 16 rnds once more (178 sts).

CHART

32	31	30	29	28	27	26	25	24	23	22	21	20	19	18	17	16	15	14	13	12	11	10	9	8	7	6	5	4	3	2	1	
•			O	/	•	•	•	•	•	•				O	/		O	/		O	/	•	•	•	•	•	•		O	/	•	16
•	\	O			•	•	•	•	•	•	\	O		\	O		\	O		•	•	•	•	•	•	\	O		•	15
•			O	/	•	•	•	•	•	•				O	/		O	/		O	/	•	•	•	•	•	•		O	/	•	14
•	\	O			•	•	•	•	•	•	\	O		\	O		\	O		•	•	•	•	•	•	\	O		•	13
•			O	/	•	•			O					/		\				O			•	•		O	/	•	4
•	\	O			•	•		O				/			\			O			•	•	\	O		•	3
•			O	/	•	•		O				/			\			O			•	•	O	/	•	2
•	\	O			•	•	O					/				\	O			•	•	\	O		•	1
32	31	30	29	28	27	26	25	24	23	22	21	20	19	18	17	16	15	14	13	12	11	10	9	8	7	6	5	4	3	2	1	

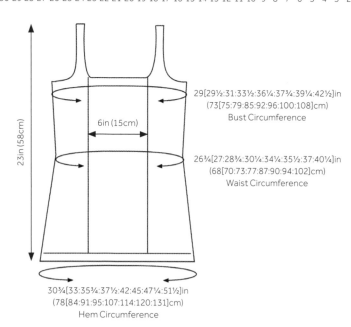

23in (58cm)

6in (15cm)

29[29½:31:33½:36¼:37¾:39¼:42½]in (73[75:79:85:92:96:100:108]cm)
Bust Circumference

26¾[27:28¾:30¼:34¼:35½:37:40¼]in (68[70:73:77:87:90:94:102]cm)
Waist Circumference

30¾[33:35¾:37½:42:45:47¼:51½]in (78[84:91:95:107:114:120:131]cm)
Hem Circumference

ALL SIZES

154[158:166:178:194:202:210:226] sts.
78[80:84:90:98:102:106:114] sts
for front and
76[78:82:88:96:100:104:112] sts
for back.

Remove shaping markers.

Cont straight in patt until you have worked 4 full reps of Lilies of the Field patt, then work rnds 1-12 once more.

SET BUST DARTS

Note: These bust darts are made using Japanese short rows and are optional. If you have a very small bust, you may not need them. If you have a very full bust, you may want to add extra bust shaping. Simply repeat short rows 1-10 as many times as desired. If you are working a big bust dart on a small size garment, you may wish to leave fewer stitches between turns in order to accommodate more short rows. Turns should be made up to the outside of the nipples, not in between the nipples.

Short row 1 (RS): K to 5 sts before halfway marker, turn work to WS, hang a removable stitch marker on the working yarn at back of work, sl1p wyif. The stitch marker should be held between the slipped stitch and the next stitch.

Short row 2 (WS): P to 5 sts before beg of rnd marker, turn work to RS, hang a removable stitch marker on the working yarn at back of work, sl1p wyib. The stitch marker should be held between the slipped stitch and the next stitch.

Short row 3 (RS): K to 3 sts before gap, turn work to WS, hang a removable stitch marker on the working yarn on WS, sl1p wyif.

Short row 4 (WS): P to 3 sts before gap, turn work to RS, hang a removable stitch marker on the working yarn on WS, sl1p wyib.

Rep rows 3 and 4 once more, or more times if desired.

Short row 5 (RS): K to gap, bring working yarn to the front, pull on the stitch marker to create a loop and slip this on to the RH needle with its right leg in front (untwisted), remove stitch marker, k this loop tog with next stitch. Now rep short row 1 before working next short row.

Short row 6 (WS): P to gap, slip next st pwise, pull on stitch marker to create a loop, take this in front of the working yarn and the slipped st and slip it on to RH needle with its right leg in front (untwisted), remove stitch marker, slip the slipped st back from LH to RH

needle and ptog with the loop.
Now rep short row 2 before working
next short row.

Short row 7 (RS): Work as short row
5, but do not turn work, instead k to
next gap and repeat the same process.
Then work as short row 1 and turn.

Short row 8 (WS): As short row 7, but
working as short rows 6 and 2.

Short rows 9 and 10: As short rows
7 and 8.

Next rnd (RS): K to gap, work as for
short row 7 to close gap, cont in patt
to end of rnd.

Next rnd: K to gap, pull on stitch
marker to make a loop, pull this behind
next st and place on LH needle, remove
marker, ktog next st and loop, cont in
patt to end of rnd.

All short rows should now have been
completed and all short row stitch
markers removed.

Cont in the round in patt as set to rnd
24 of Lilies of the Field patt.

DIVIDE FOR STRAPS

SIZE 1 ONLY

Next rnd: Cast off 10 sts, k11, slip
34 Back Panel sts back to a third needle
and work as foll: work 1 st from Back
Panel tog with next st of back, slip
11 sts just worked to a holder, working
across back sts and Back Panel work
three-needle cast off over 32 sts, work
1 st from Back Panel tog with next st
of back, k11, slip 12 sts just worked to
a holder, cast off 10 sts to end of back,
cast off 5 sts, k23, slip sts just worked
to a holder, cast off 22 sts, k23, slip sts
just worked to a holder or scrap yarn,
cast off 5 sts to end of front.

SIZES 2 AND 3 ONLY

Next rnd: Cast off 11[13] sts, k11[11]
then slip sts just worked to a holder,
return 34 held sts for Back Panel to
a third needle and work three-needle
cast-off with these and next 34 sts of

back, k11[11] then slip sts just worked
to a holder, cast off 11[13] sts to end
of back, cast off 6[7] sts, k23[23], slip
sts just worked to a holder, cast off
22[24] sts, k23[23], slip sts just worked
to a holder or scrap yarn, cast off
6[7] sts – this should take you to the
end of the front sts.

SIZES 4-8 ONLY

Next rnd: Cast off 12[13:13:13:13] sts,
k13[13:15:17:19] then slip sts just
worked to a holder, cast off
2[5:5:5:7] sts, return 34 held sts for
Back Panel to a third needle and work
three-needle cast-off with these and
next 34 sts of back, cast off
2[5:5:5:7] sts, k13[13:15:17:19] then slip
sts just worked to a holder, cast off
12[13:13:13:13] sts to end of back,
cast off 7[9:9:11:11] sts,
k25[25:27:27:29], slip sts just worked
to holder, cast off 26[30:30:30:34] sts,
k25[25:27:27:29], slip sts just worked
to a holder or scrap yarn, cast off
7[9:9:11:11] sts to end of front.

ALL SIZES

Now work each strap separately.

LEFT FRONT STRAP

Slip 23[23:23:25:25:27:27:29] held sts
for Left Front Strap back to needles.
With WS facing and starting at neck
edge, rejoin yarn and p across all sts.
**Next row (RS – dec): (K1, p1)
2[2:2:3:3:3:4:4] times, ssk, k to last
6[6:6:8:8:8:10:10] sts, k2tog, (p1, k1)
2[2:2:3:3:3:4:4] times (dec 2).
Next row: (P1, k1) 2[2:2:3:3:3:4:4] times,
p to last 6[6:6:8:8:8:10:10] sts, (k1, p1)
2[2:2:3:3:3:4:4] times.
Rep last 2 rows 6[6:6:5:5:6:4:5] more
times. 9[9:9:13:13:13:17:17] sts.
Next row (RS): (K1, p1) to last st, k1.
Next row: (P1, k1) to last st, p1.
Rep last 2 rows until Strap
meas 7[7:8:8:8:8¾:8¾:9½]in

(18[18:20:20:20:22:22:24]cm) from
armhole cast off or desired length
to shoulder.
Put sts on hold.

RIGHT FRONT STRAP

Slip 23[23:23:25:25:27:27:29] held sts
for Right Front Strap back to needles.
With WS facing and starting at side
edge, rejoin yarn and p across all sts.
Work as for Left Front Strap from **
to end.

RIGHT AND LEFT BACK STRAPS (BOTH ALIKE)

Slip 11[11:11:13:13:15:17:19] held sts
back to needles and, with RS facing,
rejoin yarn.

SIZES 1, 2, 3, 6 AND 8 ONLY

Next row (RS – dec): (K1, p1)
2[2:2:3:4] times, s2kpo, (p1, k1)
2[2:2:3:4] times.
9[9:9:15:17] sts.

ALL SIZES

9[9:9:13:13:13:17:17] sts.
Next row (RS): K1, (p1, k1) to end.
Next row: P1, (k1, p1) to end.
Rep last 2 rows until Strap
meas 7[7:8:8:8:8¾:8¾:9½]in
(18[18:20:20:20:22:22:24]cm) from
armhole cast off or desired length
to shoulder.
Put sts on hold.

TO FINISH

Join straps using three-needle
cast off.

EDGINGS (OPTIONAL)

If your front and back neck edges
aren't as neat as you would like, pick
up stitches along the neck edge, then
work as foll:

Edging row (WS): P1, p2tog, cast off
to last 3 sts, p2tog tbl, cast off to end.
Weave in ends and block.

Go bananas

Unusually, this hat is knitted from the top down, starting with an i-cord for the stem and ending with ear flaps. Knit the scarf to match, then add in the brown lines using duplicate stitch or Swiss darning embroidery, which is worked just as you would to weave in ends.

SIZES

HAT
1[2:3]

To fit: Toddler[Child:Adult]

Brim circumference: 15[19:24½]in (38[48:62]cm)

Height excluding earflaps: 7[8¾:10½]in (18[22:27]cm)

Earflap length including i-cord stem: 3¼[4¼:6]in (8.5[11:15]cm)

SCARF
Width: 5½in (14cm)

Length: 49in (124cm)

Figures in square brackets refer to larger sizes: where there is only one set of figures this applies to all sizes.

YOU WILL NEED

Cascade 220 Superwash Merino
100% superwash Merino wool (approx 220yd/200m per 100g)

HAT
1 x 100g ball in 09 Lemon (A)

Small amount in 03 Rich Brown (B)

4.5mm circular needle

4.5mm double-pointed needles

Stitch markers

Stitch holder

SCARF
2 x 100g balls in 09 Lemon (A)

Small amount in 03 Rich Brown (B)

6mm needles

4.5mm double-pointed needles

Stitch marker

Note: Yarn amounts given are based on average requirements and are approximate.

TENSION
19 sts and 40 rnds to 4in (10cm) over g st using 4.5mm needle (Hat).

16 sts and 25 rows to 4in (10cm) over slip st and g st patt with 2 strands held tog using 6mm needles (Scarf).

Use larger or smaller needles if necessary to obtain correct tension.

TIP
When changing colours in i-cord, hold both colours together for the first stitch.

HAT
Using 4.5mm dpns and B, cast on 4 sts.

Work 2 rows in i-cord.

Change to A.

Work 5 rows in i-cord.

SET CROWN INCREASES
Distribute sts over 2 dpns and work as foll, changing to circular needle when necessary to accommodate sts.

Rnd 1: (Kfb) around (8 sts).

Rnd 2: (K1, m1p, p1) around (12 sts).

Rnds 3, 5 and 7: Knit.

Rnd 4: (Sl1p wyib, m1p, p2, pm) around (16 sts).

Rnd 6: (Sl1p wyib, p to m, sm) around.

Rnd 8: (Sl1p wyib, m1p, p to m, sm) around (inc 4).

Rnd 9: Knit.

Rnd 10: (Sl1p wyib, p to m, sm) around.

Rnd 11: Knit.

Rep last 4 rnds until you have 60 sts (15 sts between markers), ending after a rnd 11.

SIZES 2 AND 3 ONLY
Rnd 1 (inc): *Sl1p wyib, p1, m1p, p to last st before m, m1p, p1, sm; rep from * to end (inc 8).

Rnd 2: Knit.

Rnd 3: *Sl1p wyib, p to m, sm; rep from * around.

Rnd 4: Knit.

Rep last 4 rnds 1[2] more times, ending after rnd 4.

ALL SIZES
60[76:84] sts (15[19:21] sts between markers).

SHAPE FRONT, BACK AND SIDES
Inc rnd 1: *Sl1p wyib, p1, m1p, p to last st before m, m1p, p1, sm, sl1p wyib, p to m, sm; rep from * to end (inc 4).

Inc rnd 2: K2, m1L, k to last st before m, m1R, k1, sm, k to m, sm; rep from * to end (inc 4).

Rep last 2 rnds 0[1:3] more times. 68[88:116] sts: 19[27:37] sts each for front and back and 15[19:21] sts each for sides).

SIZES 1 AND 2 ONLY
Rep inc rnd 1 once more. 72[92]sts: 21[29] sts each for front and back and 15[19] sts each for sides.

Next rnd: Knit, slipping markers.

ALL SIZES

SET STRAIGHT SECTION

Rnd 1: (Sl1p wyib, p to m, sm) around.

Rnd 2: Knit, slipping markers.

Rep last 2 rnds until straight section meas 1¼[1½:3¼]in (3[4:8]cm).

SET RIB AND EARFLAP PATT

Next rnd: *Sl1p wyib, p2tog, (k1, p1) to m, sm, sl1p wyib, p to m, sm; rep from * to end. 70[90:114] sts.

Next rnd: *(K1, p1) to m, sm, k to m, sm; rep from * to end.

Rep last rnd until rib section meas ¾in (2cm).

SET EARFLAPS

Next rnd: Sl1p wyib, do not break A, using B cast off 19[27:35] sts kwise, break B, slip next 16[20:22] sts to holder for earflap, using B cast off 19[27:35] sts kwise, 16[20:22] sts rem on needle including st slipped at beg of rnd.

**Turn to work WS, using A.

Next row (WS): Sl1p wyif, k to last st, sl1p wyif.

Next row: Knit.

Rep last 2 rows 0[1:5] more times, then first row once more.

SET EARFLAP SHAPING

Row 1 (RS – dec): K1, ssk, k to last 3 sts, k2tog, k1 (dec 2).

Row 2: Sl1p wyif, k to last st, sl1p wyif.

Row 3: Knit.

Row 4: As row 2.

Changing to dpns where necessary, rep last 4 rows until 6 sts rem, ending after row 4.

Next row (WS): K1, ssk, k2tog, k1 (4 sts).

Do not turn work, slip sts to other end of dpn to work RS again.

Work 5 rows of i-cord.

Change to B.

Work 2 rows of i-cord.

Cast off.

SECOND EARFLAP

Return the held 16[20:22] sts to needles and, beg with a WS row, work as for first earflap from **.

TO FINISH

Using B, Swiss-darn along slip-st columns.

Weave in ends.

SCARF

Using 4.5mm dpns and B, cast on 4 sts.

Work 2 rows in i-cord.

Change to A.

Work 6 rnds in i-cord.

SET INCREASE PATT

Change to 6mm needles, join a second strand of A and cont with 2 strands held together as foll:

Row 1 (WS): Knit.

Row 2: K1, kfb, k1, pm, p1, kfb, k1 (6 sts).

Row 3: Sl1p wyif, k to 1 st before m, sl1p wyib, sm, sl1p wyif, k to last st, sl1p wyif.

Row 4: K to m, sm, p1, k to end.

Row 5: Sl1p wyif, m1L, k to 1 st before m, sl1p wyib, sm, sl1p wyif, k to last st, m1R, sl1p wyif (8 sts).

Row 6: As row 4.

Row 7: As row 3.

Row 8: As row 4.

Rep last 4 rows 7 more times (22 sts), then rep rows 7 and 8 to cont straight until Scarf meas 42in (107cm), ending after row 7.

SET DECREASE PATT

Row 1 (RS – dec): K1, ssk, k to m, sm, p1, k to last 3 sts, k2tog, k1 (20 sts).

Row 2: Sl1p wyif, k to 1 st before m, sl1p wyib, sm, sl1p wyif, k to last st, sl1p wyif.

Row 3: K to m, sm, p1, k to end.

Row 4: As row 2.

Rep last 4 rows 7 more times, ending after a row 4 (6 sts). Remove marker.

Next row (dec): K1, ssk, k2tog, k1 (4 sts).

Change to 4.5mm dpns.

With RS facing, work 6 rows in i-cord.

Change to B.

Work 2 rows in i-cord.

Cast off.

TO FINISH

Using B, Swiss-darn along slip-st columns.

Weave in ends.

Magdalene

This lightweight, three-quarter-sleeve sweater, designed to be worn as a layering piece in cooler weather or on its own when it's warmer, starts out with two matching cable panels. Stitches are picked up along the sides and knitted to a certain point, after which the two panels are joined and the sides are worked in one piece to the sleeves, which are knitted in the round, leaving no sewing up at the end.

SIZE

One size – adjustable
Chest circumference: 53½in (136cm)
Length: 21½in (54.5cm)
Sleeve length: 9¾in (25cm) folded,
12in (30cm) unfolded
Cable panel width: 9¾in (25cm)
Each 20-row cable repeat meas:
2½in (6.5cm)

YOU WILL NEED

John Arbon Yarnadelic Sport
100% Falkland Corriedale wool
(approx 364yd/333m per 100g)
4 x 100g skeins in English Sparrows
4mm needles
4mm circular needle 100cm long
3.5mm circular needle
3.5mm and 4mm double-pointed
    needles (optional – use circular
    needle for magic loop method
    if preferred)
Cable needle
Crochet hook for provisional cast on
Stitch markers
Small stitch holders or safety pins
Long stitch holders or scrap yarn
2 x ¾in (15mm) diameter buttons

Note: Yarn amounts given are based
on average requirements and
are approximate.

TENSION

24 sts and 31 rows to 4in (10cm) over
st st using 4mm needles.
*Use larger or smaller needles if
necessary to obtain correct tension.*

PATTERN NOTES

This is a loose-fitting, swingy, three-
quarter-sleeve jumper designed to be
worn over a long-sleeved top or on its
own on warmer days. It is designed to
fit a range of body sizes with more or
less positive ease.
However, it is also easy to adjust, so
take a few measurements of your body
or a favourite jumper you already own
to make sure you make this just the
way you want.
Length: To make the jumper shorter
or longer, simply add or subtract one
or more 20-row cable pattern repeat
in the initial panels.
Width: To make the jumper narrower,
once you have picked up stitches along
the cable panel and started working
sideways, skip or shorten the four-row
hem decrease section and move to
decreasing on alternate rows sooner.
To make the jumper wider, work a
longer straight section before starting
the hem decreases.
Sleeves: An easy way to lengthen
the sleeves would be to work a longer
ribbed cuff section. Alternatively you

can extend the stocking stitch section
by working more rows in between
decreases. Take care to add in full
pattern repeats so the cable pattern
ends in the right place.
Please note: If you increase the size
of this jumper I would advise buying an
extra skein of yarn. Please take note of
any alterations so you can match them
on the second side or panel.

TIP

Place markers between the different
cable panels to help you keep track.

CABLE LEFT
Worked over 4 sts and 4 rows
Row 1 (RS): Knit.
Row 2: Purl.
Row 3: C4B.
Row 4: Purl.

CABLE RIGHT
Worked over 4 sts and 4 rows
Row 1 (RS): Knit.
Row 2: Purl.
Row 3: C4F.
Row 4: Purl.

CLUSTER RIB BODY
Worked over 5 sts and 20 rows
Row 1 (RS): (P1, k1 tbl) twice, p1.
Row 2: (K1, p1 tbl) twice, k1.
Rows 3 and 4: As rows 1 and 2.

Row 5: P1, cl3, p1.
Rows 6 and 8: K1, p3, k1.
Row 7: P1, k3, p1.
Row 9: As row 5.
Row 10: As row 2.
Rows 11–20: As rows 1 and 2.

CLUSTER RIB SHOULDER
Worked over 5 sts and 12 rows
Row 1 (RS): (P1, k1 tbl) twice, p1.
Row 2: (K1, p1 tbl) twice, k1.
Rows 3 and 4: As rows 1 and 2.
Row 5: P1, cl3, p1.
Rows 6 and 8: K1, p3, k1.
Row 7: P1, k3, p1.
Row 9: As row 5.
Row 10: K1, p1, k1 tbl, p1, k1.
Rows 11 and 12: As rows 1 and 2.

CLUSTER RIB IN THE ROUND
Worked over 5 sts and 12 rnds
Rnds 1–4: (P1, k1 tbl) twice, p1.
Rnd 5: P1, cl3, p1.
Rnds 6–8: P1, k3, p1.
Rnd 9: As rnd 5.
Rnd 10: P1, k1, p1 tbl, k1, p1.
Rnds 11 and 12: As rnd 1.

LEAF PANEL
Starts and ends with 7 sts and 20 rows
Row 1 (RS): P3, kyokyok, p3 (11 sts).
Row 2: K3, p5, k3.
Rows 3–9: Work each st as it appears.
Row 10: K3, p5tog, k3 (7 sts).
Row 11: Purl.
Rows 12–14: Work each st as it appears.
Row 15: P3, kyok, p3 (9 sts).
Rows 16 and 17: Work each st as it appears.
Row 18: K3, p3tog, k3 (7 sts).
Rows 19 and 20: Purl.

CENTRE CABLE WORKED BACK AND FORTH
Worked over 16 sts and 10 rows
Row 1 (RS): K1, (p2, k2) 3 times, p2, k1.

Rows 2–6: Work each st as it appears.
Row 7: C8Brib, C8Frib.
Rows 8–10: Work each st as it appears.

CENTRE CABLE WORKED IN THE ROUND
Worked over 16 sts and 12 rnds
Rnd 1: K1, (p2, k2) 3 times, p2, k1.
Rnds 2–6: As rnd 1.
Rnd 7: C8Brib, C8Frib.
Rnds 8–12: As rnd 1.

CABLE PANEL (MAKE 2)
Using scrap yarn and the crochet provisional cast on, cast on 3 sts to a double-pointed 4mm needle. Change to main yarn.
Row 1: Knit.
Row 2: Slide sts to other end of needle and k the same side again.
Cont in i-cord as set by rows 1 and 2 until you have worked a total of 74 rows.
Next row: K1, kfb, k1 (4 sts).
Slip last st worked to a needle and rem 3 sts to a small holder or safety pin. Using 4mm needles pick up and k73 sts along i-cord edge, 1 st in each st (74 sts).
SET CABLE PATTERN
Set-up row (WS): K3, p4, k2, (k1, p1 tbl) twice, k3, p4, k9, p1, (k2, p2) 3 times, k2, p1, k9, p4, k2, (k1, p1 tbl) twice, k3, p4, k3.
Working from written instructions or Body Panel Chart, work as foll:
Row 1 (RS): P3, work row 1 of Cable Left over next 4 sts, p2, work row 1 of Cluster Rib over next 5 sts, p2, work row 1 of Cable Left over next 4 sts, p2, work row 1 of Leaf Panel over next 7 sts, work row 1 of Centre Cable over next 16 sts, work row 1 of Leaf Panel over next 7 sts, p2, work row 1 of Cable Right over next 4 sts, p2, work row 1 of Cluster Rib over next 5 sts, p2, work row 1 of Cable Right over next 4 sts, p3.
Row 2: K3, work row 2 of Cable Right,

k2, work row 2 of Cluster Rib, k2, work row 2 of Cable Right, k2, work row 2 of Leaf Panel, work row 2 of Centre Cable, work row 2 of Leaf Panel, k2, work row 2 of Cable Left, k2, work row 2 of Cluster Rib, k2, work row 2 of Cable Left, k3.
These 2 rows set patt. Cont in patt as set until you have worked 8 full reps of main cable patt, ending with row 20. Slip sts on to a long holder or scrap yarn.
SET SIDE PANELS
With RS facing, starting at bottom edge of piece, slip 3 i-cord sts from short holder to needles, then pick up and k129 sts (132 sts).
Row 1 (WS): P to last 3 sts, sl3 wyif.
Row 2: Knit.
Rep these 2 rows 3 more times (8 rows total).
Slip sts on to a long holder or scrap yarn. With RS facing, turn piece to other side and, starting at neck edge, pick up and k129 sts along side edge, then slip 3 held i-cord sts to needle (132 sts).
Row 1 (WS): Sl3 wyif, p to end.
Row 2: Knit.
Rep these 2 rows 3 more times (8 rows total).
Slip sts to a long holder or scrap yarn. Set aside.

SIDE AND SLEEVE (BOTH SIDES ALIKE)
Lay both panels out with neck edges (stitches on hold) together and slip both sets of sts on one side to long circular needle. You will be working up one side, across the shoulder and down the other side, starting and ending with the i-cord edge.
With RS facing, work as foll:
Set-up row 1 (RS): K to last 2 sts of first set of sts, sk2po (ktog last st of first set of sts and first st of second set of sts, then psso), k to end (262 sts).

SHOULDER PANEL CHART

KEY

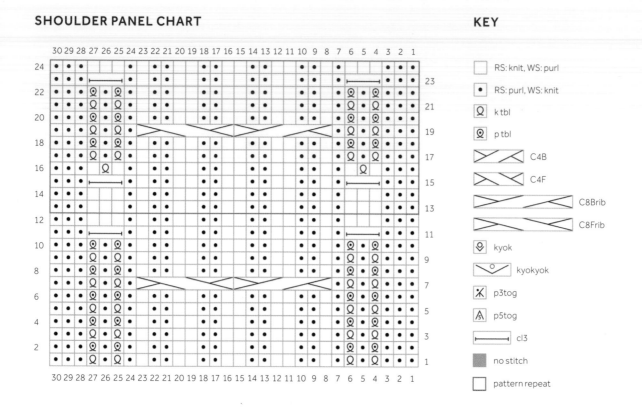

	RS: knit, WS: purl
•	RS: purl, WS: knit
Ⓠ	k tbl
Ⓠ	p tbl
⤬	C4B
⤬	C4F
⤬	C8Brib
⤬	C8Frib
Ⓠ	kyok
⤵	kyokyok
⤬	p3tog
Ⓐ	p5tog
⊢—⊣	cl3
▨	no stitch
⬜	pattern repeat

BODY PANEL CHART

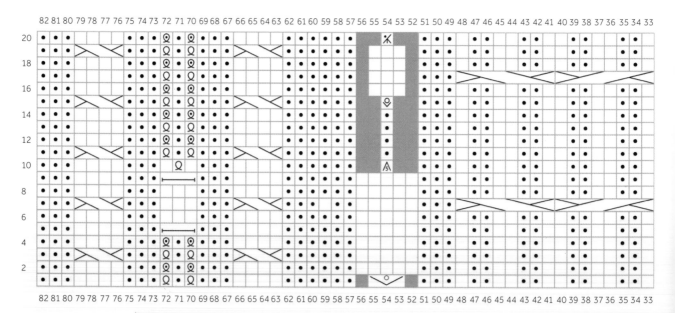

SLEEVE PANEL CHART

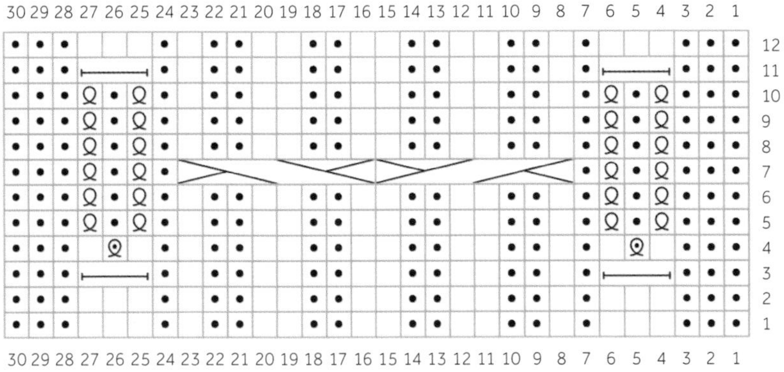

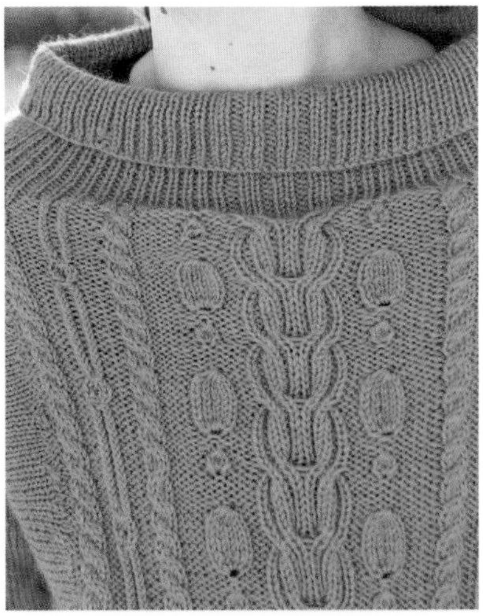

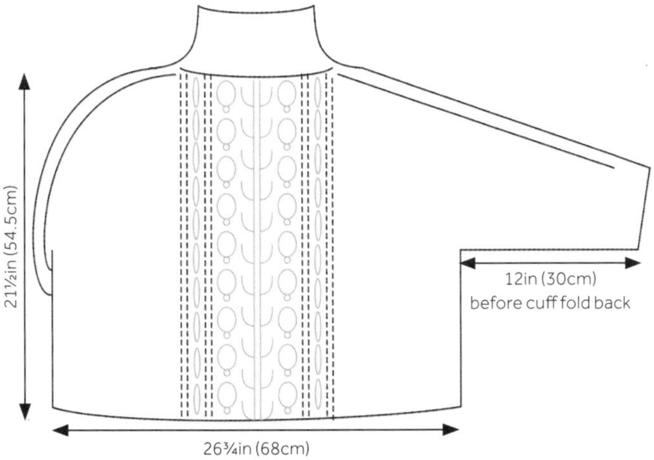
21½in (54.5cm)
12in (30cm)
before cuff fold back
26¾in (68cm)

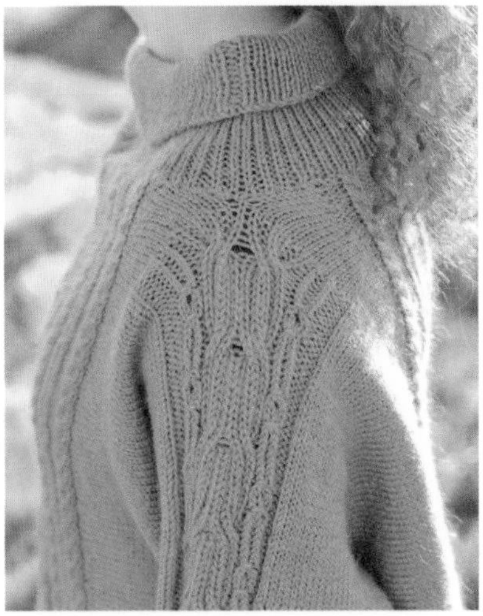

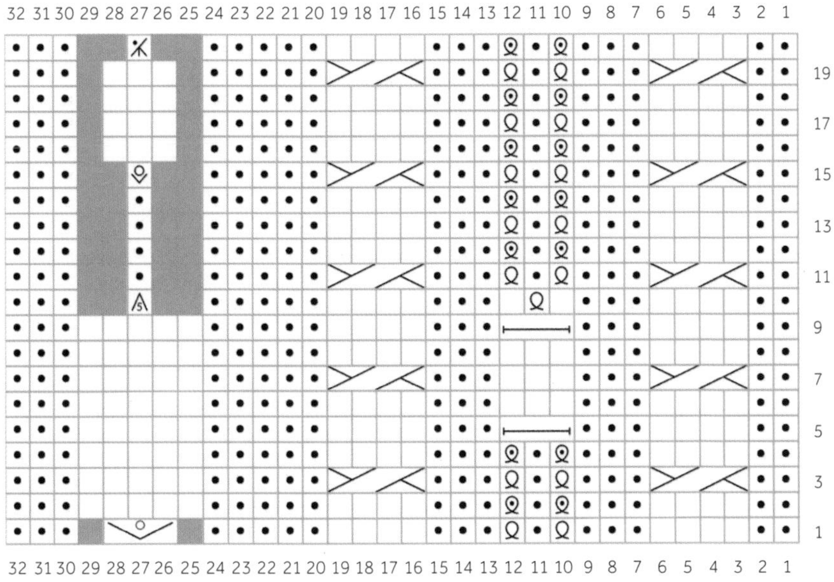

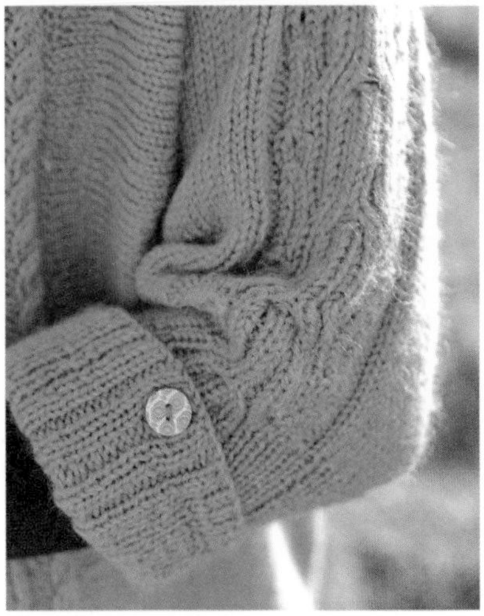

Set-up row 2: Sl3 wyif, p to last 3 sts, sl3 wyif.

Set-up row 3: K116, pm, k30, pm, k to end.

Set-up row 4: Sl3 wyif, p to m, sm, k2, (k1, p1) 3 times, (k2, p2) 3 times, k2, (p1, k1) 3 times, k2, sm, p to last 3 sts, sl3 wyif.

SET PATT AND HEM DECREASES

Note: Read all of next section before starting.

Working from written instructions or Shoulder Panel Chart, work as foll:

Row 1 (RS): K to m, sm, p2, work row 1 of Cluster Rib Shoulder patt over next 5 sts, work row 1 of Centre Cable over next 16 sts, work row 1 of Cluster Rib Shoulder patt over next 5 sts, p2, sm, k to end.

Row 2: Sl3 wyif, p to m, sm, k2, work row 2 of Cluster Rib Shoulder patt over next sts, work row 2 of Centre Cable over next 16 sts, work row 2 of Cluster Rib Shoulder patt over next 5 sts, k2, sm, p to last 3 sts, sl3 wyif.

These 2 rows form patt. For Cluster Rib rep rows 1 and 2 twice more, then start from row 1 and cont in patt throughout. For Centre Cable cont working through patt as set (see Chart).

AT THE SAME TIME work hem decreases as foll:

Work next 2 rows without shaping.

Next row (dec): K4, ssk, patt as set to last 6 sts, k2tog, k4.

Rep dec row every 4th row until you have worked 3 full 12-row patt reps (246 sts).

Then work dec row on every RS row and work one more full patt rep, then rows 1 and 2 again (234 sts).

SHAPE SIDE

Set-up row (RS): Sssk, k59, pm, k to m,

sm, patt to m, sm, k40, pm, k to last 3 sts, k3tog (230 sts).

Fold garment in half with right sides together and stitches parallel to each other with both tips facing right ready to be knitted. Use a third needle to work three-needle cast off as foll: K tog 1 st from front needle with 1 st from back needle, *k tog next st from front needle with next st from back needle, pass first st on RH needle over second st on RH needle (1 st cast off); rep from * until you have reached the underarm markers placed on the last row. You have cast off 60 sts on each side and joined the two sides together. Remove markers. Cast off 1 more st from each side (109 sts).

Slip last st on RH needle to LH needle. Turn piece RS out.

SLEEVE

Working from written instructions or Sleeve Chart, cont in the round as set by Shoulder Chart on dpns or on circular needle using the magic loop method.

Set-up rnd: Pm, patt to last 2 sts, k2tog (108 sts).

Rnd 1 (dec): K1, k2tog, k to m, sm, patt to m, sm, k to last 3 sts, k2tog, k1 (106 sts).

Work 3 rnds straight in patt as set.

Rep rnds 1-4 another 10 times, then work dec rnd once more (84 sts).

SET CUFF

Change to 3.5mm dpns or circular needle.

Rnd 1: (K1, p1) to 1 st before m, k1, remove m, (p1, k1) 3 times, p1, pm, work Centre Cable over next 16 sts, pm, (p1, k1) 3 times, p1, remove marker, (k1, p1) to last st, k1.

Rnd 2: Rib to m, sm, patt to m, sm, rib to end.

Rnd 3: As rnd 2.

Rnd 4: K1, rib 2 tog, rib to m, sm, patt to m, sm, rib to last 3 sts, rib 2tog, k1 (82 sts).

Now cont in rib and Centre Cable patt as set but do not work cable rnd (rnd 7) again.

Rep dec rnd every 4th rnd 3 more times, keeping rib correct as set (76 sts).

Cont straight in rib and Centre Cable patt as set, without working cable rnd, until cuff meas 5in (13cm).

Buttonhole rnd: Rib to m, sm, k1, p2, k2, p2, yo, k2tog, p2, k2, p2, k1, sm, rib to end.

Work 6 more rnds in rib and Centre Cable patt as set.

Cast off.

Work second side to match first.

NECK

Slip held sts for neckline to 3.5mm circular needle.

Set-up rnd: Beg at one side, *pm, pick up and k8 sts, working across first set of neckline sts (k1, p1) 13 times, k2tog, p1, pm, work Centre Cable in the Round over next 16 sts, pm, p1, k2tog, (p1, k1) 13 times, pick up and k8 sts; rep from * once (176 sts – 88 each for back and front).

Rib rnd: *Sm, (k1, p1) to m, sm, patt to m, sm, (p1, k1) to m; rep from * once more. Rep rib rnd until neck meas 5in (13cm) or desired length.

Cast off loosely.

TO FINISH

Pin out to measurements, cover with a damp cloth and leave to dry.

Weave in ends. Sew buttons just below last cable cross on Sleeves, fold over cuffs to button.

Pete's owls

This pattern came into being when my friend Peter – modelling here – asked me to recreate a favourite jumper which had fallen apart. Taking inspiration from the original and adding in a gorgeous Scottish heritage wool and some cute cabled owls, I designed this sweater, which is knitted from the bottom up in the round. Sleeves are knitted separately to the underarms and then the yoke is worked all in one piece.

SIZES

To fit: S[M:L:XL:2XL:3XL]

To fit chest circumference:
34-36[38-40:42-44:46-48:50-52:
54-56]in (86-92[97-102:107-112:
117-122:127-132:127-142]cm)

Actual chest:
37¾[41¾:45¾:49½:53½:57½]in
(96[106:116:126:136:146]cm)

Length from underarm: 18¼in (46cm)

Length from shoulder:
26[26¾:27¼:27½:28:28¼]in
(66[68:69:70:71:72]cm)

Sleeve length: 18¼in (46cm)

Figures in square brackets refer to larger sizes: where there is only one set of figures this applies to all sizes.

YOU WILL NEED

New Lanark Chunky 100% wool
(approx 131yd/120m per 100g)
6[7:7:8:9:10] x 100g balls in Denim
7mm and 8mm circular needles
7mm and 8mm double-pointed
  needles (optional)
Cable needle
Stitch markers
Stitch holders or scrap yarn

Note: Yarn amounts given are based on average requirements and are approximate.

TENSION

12 sts and 20 rnds to 4in (10cm) over g st using 8mm needles.
Use larger or smaller needles if necessary to obtain correct tension.

PATTERN NOTES

When slipping stitches, always hold yarn at back of work.
Body and Sleeves must end on same rnd of Owl Patt. Make a note of this rnd so you can be sure to end on the same rnd and will know with which rnd to start the Yoke.
When shaping Yoke, continue working in Owl Patt until you can no longer complete the pattern, then rep rnd 2 of Owl Patt over rem patt sts as set.
Pete is wearing size 1.

OWL PATTERN

Worked over 12 sts and 16 rnds
Rnd 1: P2, C4B, C4F, p2.
Rnd 2: P2, k8, p2.
Rnds 3 and 4: As rnd 2.
Rnd 5: As rnd 1.
Rnds 6 and 7: As rnd 2.
Rnds 8, 10, 12 and 14: P2, k2, p4, k2, p2.
Rnds 9, 11, 13, 15 and 16: As rnd 2.

BODY

Using 7mm needle, cast on
124[136:148:160:172:184] sts.

Join to work in the round, taking care not to twist sts, and pm to mark beg of rnd.
Rib rnd: (K1, p1) around.
Rep rib rnd 4 more times.
Change to 8mm needle.
Knit 1 rnd.

SET MAIN PATTERN

SIZES 1, 3 AND 5 ONLY
Rnd 1: *Sl1p, (p5, sl1p) 2[3:4] times, pm, work rnd 1 of Owl Patt over next 12 sts, pm, (sl1p, p5) twice, sl1p, pm, work rnd 1 of Owl Patt over next 12 sts, pm, (sl1p, p5) 2[3:4] times, pm for side; rep from * once more.

SIZES 2, 4 AND 6 ONLY
Rnd 1: *K3, sl1p, (p5, sl1p) 2[3:4] times, pm, work rnd 1 of Owl Patt over next 12 sts, pm, (sl1p, p5) twice, sl1p, pm, work rnd 1 of Owl Patt over next 12 sts, pm, (sl1p, p5) 2[3:4] times, sl1p, k2, pm for side; rep from * once more.

ALL SIZES
Rnd 2: *K to m, sm, work rnd 2 of Owl Patt over next 12 sts, sm; rep from * to end of last Owl Patt, k to end.
Rnd 3: K0[3:0:3:0:3], sl1p, (p5, sl1p) 2[2:3:3:4:4] times, sm, work rnd 3 of Owl Patt over next 12 sts, sm, (sl1p, p5) twice, sl1p, pm, work rnd 3 of Owl Patt over next 12 sts, pm, (sl1p, p5) 2[2:3:3:4:4] times, -[sl1p:-:sl1p:-:sl1p], k0[2:0:2:0:2], sm; rep from * once more.

These 2 rnds set position of garter slip stitch patt and Owl Patt. Cont in patt as set until piece meas 18¼in (46cm), ending with an odd-numbered rnd. Set aside.

SLEEVES (MAKE 2)

Using 7mm needle cast on 32 sts. Join to work in the round, taking care not to twist sts, and pm to mark beg of rnd.

Work 5 rnds in rib as for Body, inc 1 st on final rnd (33 sts).

Change to 8mm needle.

Knit 1 rnd.

SET MAIN PATT

Rnd 1: Sl1p, p9, sl1p, pm, work Owl Patt rnd 1 over next 12 sts, pm, sl1p, p to end.

Rnd 2: K to m, sm, work Owl Patt rnd 2 over next 12 sts, sm, k to end.

Keeping Owl Patt correct, rep rnds 1 and 2 three more times, then rnd 1 again.

Next rnd (inc): K1, m1L, patt as set (Owl Patt rnd 10) to end, m1R (35 sts).

Cont as set, working inc rnd every 10th[8th:8th:6th:6th:4th] rnd a total of 4[7:8:10:12:14] times, taking inc sts into g st patt. 41[47:49:53:57:61] sts.

Cont straight until Sleeve meas 18¼in (46cm), ending with an odd-numbered rnd.

Slip 4 sts at beg of rnd and 3 sts at end of rnd on to a holder (7 sts total). 34[40:42:46:50:54] sts rem for Sleeve. Set aside.

YOKE

JOIN BODY AND SLEEVES

Note: Beg and end of rnd will be at back right shoulder. Slip 4 sts to a holder, pm1, patt across Body as set to 3 sts before side marker, slip these sts and 4 foll sts to a holder (7 sts on holder), pm2, patt as set across

34[40:42:46:50:54] sts held for left Sleeve, pm3, patt across Body to last 3 sts, slip these 3 sts to same holder as first 4 sts of rnd (7 sts on holder), pm4, patt across 34[40:42:46:50:54] sts held for right Sleeve. 178[202:218:238:258:278] sts: 55[61:67:73:79:85] for back and front and 34[40:42:46:50:54] sts for each Sleeve.

Next rnd: *Sm, p1, k1, patt as set to 2 sts before m, k1, p1, sm, k1, p1, k1, patt as set to 3 sts before m, k1, p1, k1; rep from * to end.

SET YOKE DECREASES

Rnd 1 (dec): *Sm, p1, k1, ssk, patt as set to 4 sts before m, k2tog, k1, p1, sm, sl1p, p1, k1, ssk, patt as set to 5 sts before m, k2tog, k1, p1, sl1p, sm; rep from * (dec 8).

Rnd 2: *Sm, p1, k2, patt as set to 3 sts before m, k2, p1, sm, k1, p1, k2, patt as set to 4 sts before m, k2, p1, k1; rep from * to end.

Rnd 3: *Sm, p1, k2, patt as set to 3 sts before m, k2, p1, sm, sl1p, p1, k2, patt as set to 4 sts before m, k2, p1, sl1p; rep from * to end.

Rnd 4: As rnd 2.

Rep last 4 rnds 5[4:3:2:1:0] more times. 130[162:186:214:242:270] sts.

Then rep dec rnd every alt rnd 7[11:14:21:24] times. 74[74:74:70:74:78] sts.

SIZES 1-3 ONLY

Next rnd (dec): *Sm, p1, k1, ssk, patt as set to 4 sts before m, k2tog, k1, p1, sm, sl1p, p1, ssk, k2tog, p1, sl1p; rep from * to end. 66[66:66] sts.

Next rnd: *Sm, p1, k2, patt as set to 3 sts before m, k2, p1, sm, k1, p1, k2, p1, k1; rep from * to end.

ALL SIZES

66[66:66:70:74:78] sts.

BACK NECK ELEVATION (OPTIONAL)

Short row 1 (RS): Patt as set across back and left Sleeve to m3, sm, p1, k1, w&t.

Short row 2 (WS): P1, k1, sm, p1, k1, p to last 2 sts before m, k1, p1, sm, k1, p1, work each rem st in Owl Patt as it appears (k the k sts and p the p sts), sm (end of Owl Patt), p to Owl Patt m, sm, work each rem st in Owl Patt as it appears to 2 sts before beg of rnd m, p1, k1, sm, sl1p wyif, k1, patt as set across right Sleeve to 2 sts before m4, k1, sl1p wyif, sm, k1, p1, w&t.

Short row 3 (RS): Patt as set to 1 st before wrapped st, w&t.

Short row 4 (WS): Patt as set by short row 2 to 1 st before wrapped st, w&t.

Short row 5: Patt as set to end of rnd.

Note: On next rnd, work wraps tog with wrapped sts in patt.

NECKBAND

Change to 7mm needle. Remove all stitch markers except for beg of rnd marker.

SIZES 1-5 ONLY

Dec rnd: *K2tog, p1, (k1, p1) 15[15:15:16:17] times; rep from * once more. 64[64:64:68:72] sts.

SIZE 6 ONLY

Dec rnd: *K2tog, p1, (k1, p1) 5 times; rep from * 5 more times (72 sts).

ALL SIZES

64[64:64:68:72:72] sts.

Rib rnd: (K1, p1) around.

Rep rib rnd 4 more times.

Cast off loosely using 8mm needle.

TO FINISH

Graft underarm sts together and weave in ends.

Block to measurements.

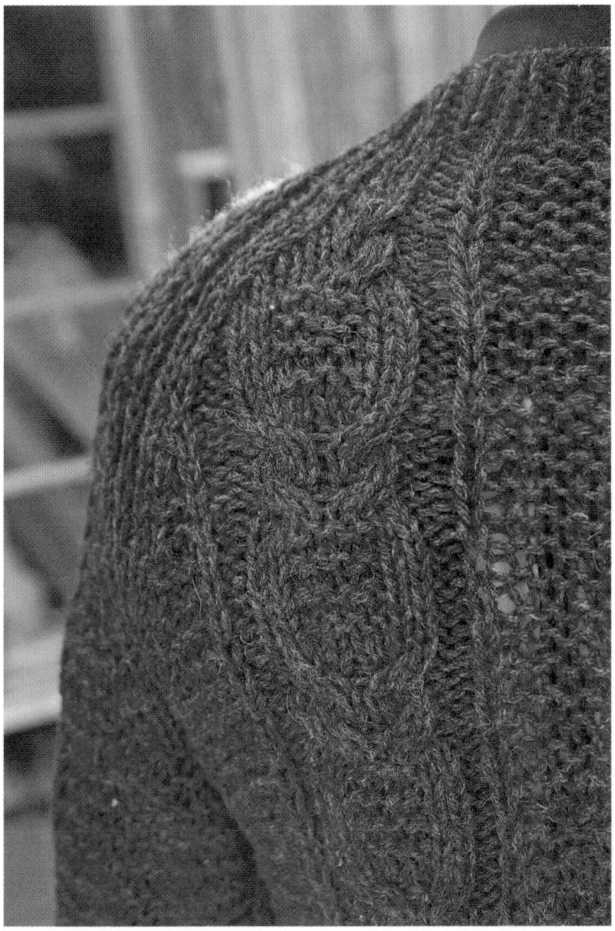

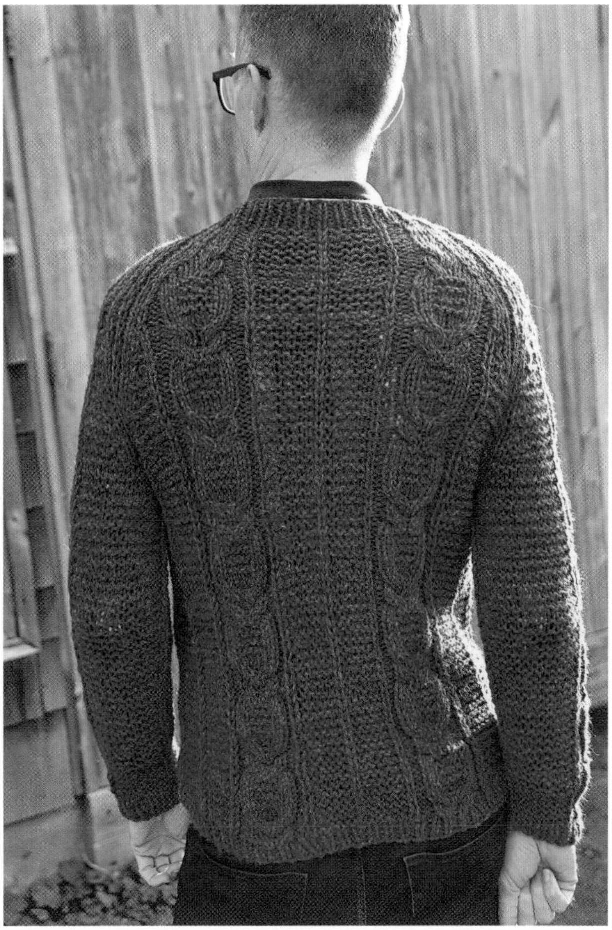

OWL PATTERN

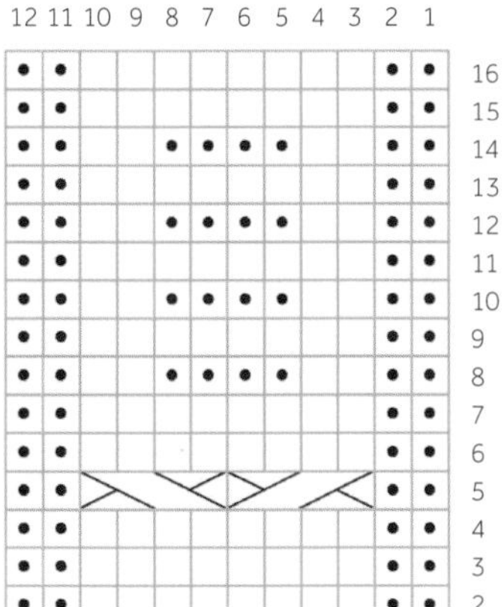
12 11 10 9 8 7 6 5 4 3 2 1
16
15
14
13
12
11
10
9
8
7
6
5
4
3
2
1
12 11 10 9 8 7 6 5 4 3 2 1

KEY

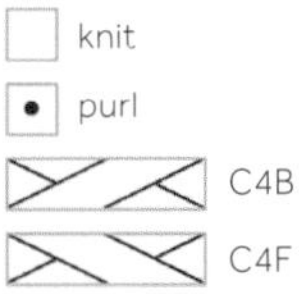
knit
purl
C4B
C4F

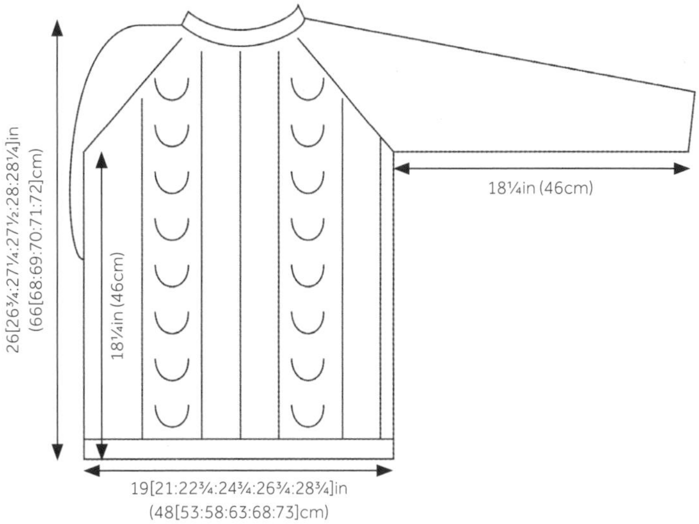
26[26¾:27¼:27½:28:28¼]in
(66[68:69:70:71:72]cm)
18¼in (46cm)
18¼in (46cm)
19[21:22¾:24¾:26¾:28¾]in
(48[53:58:63:68:73]cm)

Elskling

Elskling means 'love' or 'darling' in Norwegian, and is the perfect name for this cute but classic top-down cabled cardigan for tiny tots. Norway was my lockdown obsession during the Covid-19 pandemic and I spent many hours learning the language on an app on my phone, so that I can now say to you: Jeg elsker deg!

SIZES

To fit age: 6[12:18:24] mths
Chest circumference:
19¾[22:23¼:25½]in (50[56:59:65]cm)
Length: 10¼[10½:11:11½]in
(26[27:28:29]cm)
Sleeve length: 4¾[5:5½:6]in)
(12[13:14:15]cm)
Figures in square brackets refer to larger sizes: where there is only one set of figures this applies to all sizes.

YOU WILL NEED

Cascade 220 Superwash Merino
100% superwash Merino wool
(approx 220yd/200m per 100g)
2[2:2:3] x 100g balls in 56
Seafoam Green
4mm and 4.5mm circular needles
4mm and 4.5mm double-pointed
    needles (optional)
Cable needle
Stitch markers
Stitch holders
4[4:5:5] x ¾in (15mm) diameter buttons

Note: Yarn amounts given are based on average requirements and are approximate.

TENSION

20 sts and 28 rows to 4in (10cm) over st st using 4.5mm needle.
25 sts and 25 rows to 4in (10cm) over cable patt using 4.5mm needle.

Heart Cable meas 3¼ x 1½in
(8 x 4cm) after blocking
Use larger or smaller needles if necessary to obtain correct tension.

HEART CABLE

Worked over 20 sts and 10 rows
Row 1 (RS): P2, C4Bp, C4F, C4B, C4Fp, p2.
Rows 2 and 4: K2, p2, k4, p4, k4, p2, k2.
Row 3: P2, k2, p4, C4B, p4, k2, p2.
Row 5: P2, C3Fp, p3, k4, p3, C3Bp, p2.
Row 6: K3, p2, k3, p4, k3, p2, k3.
Row 7: P3, C3Fp, p2, C4B, p2, C3Bp, p3.
Row 8: K4, p2, k2, p4, k2, p2, k4.
Row 9: P4, C4Fp, k4, C4Bp, p4.
Row 10: K4, p12, k4.
These 10 rows form Cable Heart patt and are repeated.

CARDIGAN

Cast on 42 sts using 4.5mm circular needle.
Set-up row 1 (RS): K3, pm (right front), k6, pm (right Sleeve), k24, pm (back), k6, pm (left Sleeve), k3 (left front).
Set-up row 2: Purl.
Set-up row 3: K1, m1R, k2, *sm, k2, m1L, k to 2 sts before m, m1R, k2; rep from * twice more, sm, k2, m1L, k1 (inc 8 – 50 sts).
Set-up row 4: Purl.
Set-up row 5: *K2, m2, k2*, sm, (k2, m1L, k to 2 sts before m, m1R, k2)

3 times, sm; rep from * to * once more (inc 10 – 60 sts).
Set-up row 6: P2, k2, p to last 4 sts, k2, p2.

SET YOKE INCREASE PATTERN

Row 1 (RS): K2, p to 2 sts before m, m1Rp, k2, *sm, k2, m1L, k to 2 sts before m, m1R, k2; rep from * twice more, k2, m1Lp, p to last 2 sts, k2 (inc 8 – 68 sts).
Row 2: P2, k to 2 sts before m, p2, sm, p to next front, sm, p2, k to last 2 sts, p2.
Row 3: K2, m1Lp, p to 2 sts before m, m1Rp, k2, *sm, k2, m1L, k to 2 sts before m, m1R, k2; rep from * twice more, k2, m1Lp, p to last 2 sts, m1Rp, k2 (inc 10 – 78 sts).
Row 4: As row 2.
Rows 5-9: Rep rows 1-4 once more, then row 1 again (104 sts).

SET CABLE TWIST

Row 10 (WS): P2, k4, pm, p4, pm, k to 2 sts before m, p2, sm, p to second front, p2, k1, pm, p4, pm, k to last 2 sts, p2.
Row 11 (RS): *K2, m1Lp, p to m, sm, C4B, sm, p to last 2 sts, m1Rp, k2*, **sm, k2, m1L, k to 2 sts before m, m1R, k2; rep from ** twice more, rep from * to * (114 sts).
Row 12: *P2, k to m, sm, p4, sm, k to 2 sts before m, p2*, sm, p to next front, sm; rep from * to *.
Cont working inc patt as set and AT THE SAME TIME work cable as for row 11 on every 4th row (so rows 15 and 19)

until you have worked row 23, a RS row (168 sts).

SET HEART CABLE
Remove cable markers on each front.

SIZE 1 ONLY
Next row (WS): P2, pm, work row 10 of Heart Cable over next 12 sts, pm, p2, sm, p to right front slipping markers, p2, sm, work row 10 of Heart Cable over next 12 sts, sm, p2.

Next row (RS): K2, sm, work row 1 of Heart Cable over next 12 sts, pm, k2, sm, k to left front slipping markers, k2, pm, work row 1 of Heart Cable over next 12 sts, pm, k2.

Next row: P to m, work row 2 of Heart Cable over next 12 sts, sm, p2, sm, p to right front slipping markers, p2, sm, work row 2 of Heart Cable over next 12 sts, sm, p2.

These rows set position of Heart Cable on right and left fronts and st st across back and Sleeves.

Work 2 more rows in patt as set.

SIZES 2, 3 AND 4 ONLY
Next row (WS): P2, pm, work row 10 of Heart Cable over next 12 sts, pm, p2, sm, p to right front slipping markers, p2, pm, work row 2 of Heart Cable over next 12 sts, pm, p to end.

Next row (RS): K2, m1L, sm, work row 1 of Heart Cable over next 12 sts, sm, m1R, k2, (sm, k2, m1L, k to last 2 sts before m, m1R, k2) 3 times, sm, k2, m1L, sm, work row 1 of Heart Cable over next 12 sts, sm, m1R, k2 (178 sts).

Next row: P to m, work row 2 of Heart Cable over next 12 sts, sm, p2, sm, p to right front slipping markers, p to m, sm, work row 2 of Heart Cable over next 12 sts, sm, p to end.

These rows set position of Heart Cable on right and left fronts and st st across back and Sleeves.

Next row (RS): K2, sm, patt to m, sm, k to last 2 sts before m, m1R, k2, (sm, k2,

m1L, k to last 2 sts before m, m1R, k2) 3 times, sm, k2, m1L, sm, patt to m, sm, k2 (186 sts).

Next row: Patt as set.

SIZE 2 ONLY
Work 2 more rows straight in patt as set.

SIZES 3 AND 4 ONLY
Next row (RS): K2, m1L, k to m, sm, patt to m, sm, k to 2 sts before m, m1R, k2, (sm, k2, m1L, k to last 2 sts before m, m1R, k2) 3 times, sm, k2, m1L, k to m, sm, patt to m, sm, k to last 2 sts, m1R, k2 (196 sts).

Next row: Patt as set.

SIZE 3 ONLY
Work 2 more rows in patt as set.

SIZE 4 ONLY
Next row (RS): K to m, sm, patt to m, sm, k to last 2 sts before m, m1R, k2, (sm, k2, m1L, k to last 2 sts before m, m1R, k2) 3 times, sm, k2, m1L, sm, patt to m, sm, k to end (204 sts).

Next row: Patt as set.

Rep last 2 rows once more (212 sts).

ALL SIZES
168[186:196:212] sts.

DIVIDE FOR BODY AND SLEEVES
Set-up row (RS): Patt to first Sleeve marker, slip next 34[38:40:44] sts to a

holder for left Sleeve, cast on 4 sts for underarm, k across 52[56:58:62] sts for back, slip next 34[38:40:44] sts to a holder for right Sleeve, cast on 4 sts for underarm, patt to end.

BODY
108[118:124:132] sts.

Cont straight in patt until you have worked 3[3:4:4] full reps of Heart Cable, then rows 1 and 2 again.

Piece meas 9[9¾:10½:11¼]in (23[24.5:27:28.5]cm), ending with a WS row.

SET RIB
Change to 4mm needle.

Next row (RS): P0[1:0:0], (k1, p1) 5[5:6:6] times, C4B, pm, (p1, k1) to 1 st before start of next Heart Cable, dec 1 if necessary so you can keep rib correct but work k1 next, (k1, p1) 4 times, C4B, pm, (p1, k1) to end[last st:end:end], p0[1:0:0].

Next row: *Rib to m, p4; rep from * once more, rib to end.

Next row: *Rib to 4 sts before m, k4, sm; rep from * once more, rib to end.

Next row: *Rib to m, p4; rep from * once more, rib to end.

Rep last 2 rows until rib meas 1in (2.5cm). Cast off.

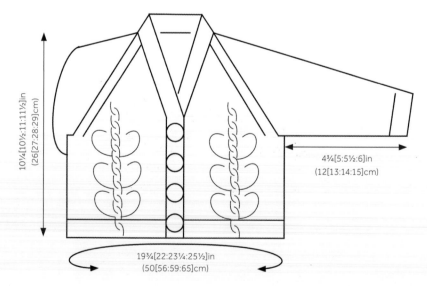

10¼[10½:11:11½]in (26[27:28:29]cm)

4¾[5:5½:6]in (12[13:14:15]cm)

19¾[22:23¼:25½]in (50[56:59:65]cm)

SLEEVES (MAKE 2)

Return 34[38:40:44] held sts to 4.5mm circular or double-pointed needles, then pick up and k1 st in each of the 4 cast-on sts at underarm, pm at centre of cast-on sts for beg of rnd. 38[42:44:48] sts.

Knit 8[4:8:10] rnds.

Next rnd (dec): K1, ssk, k to last 3 sts, k2tog, k1 (dec 2).

Knit 1[2:2:2] rnds.

Rep last 2[3:3:3] rnds 8[9:9:10] more times. 20[22:24:26] sts.

SET CUFF

Change to 4mm needle.

Next rnd: (K1, p1) around.

Rep rib rnd 7 more times.

Cast off loosely.

BUTTON AND BUTTONHOLE BAND

With RS facing, starting at bottom left corner of front opening, pick up and k26[28:36:38] sts up left front side, 12[14:16:18] sts up left neck slope, 35 sts across back neck, 12[14:16:18] sts down right neck slope, 26[28:36:38] sts down right front side. 111[119:139:147] sts.

Row 1 (WS): (K1, p1) to last st, k1.

Row 2: (P1, k1) to last st, k1.

Row 3 (WS – buttonholes): K1, p1, *k2tog, yo, (k1, p1) 4 times; rep from * 2[2:3:3] more times, k2tog, yo, (k1, p1) to last st, k1.

Row 4: As row 2.

Rep row 1 once more.

Cast off in rib.

TO FINISH

Sew on buttons to match buttonholes.

Weave in ends.

Block.

LUX

Light shines through the eyelets in this pretty lace pattern and a lighter shade shines through the turquoise tone of this lovely lightweight but chunky yarn. This shrug is knitted from the centre out, starting with the central lace panel, then picking up stitches and working outwards to the cuffs, so you can make it to exactly the length and width you want.

SIZES

To fit: S-M[M-L:L-XL]

Length at centre back:
14¼[15¾:17¼]in (36[40:44]cm)

Full width (adjustable):
51¼[54¼:57½]in (130[138:146]cm)

Cuff length (adjustable): 14¼in (36cm)

Figures in square brackets refer to larger sizes: where there is only one set of figures this applies to all sizes.

YOU WILL NEED

Cascade Yarns Cantata

70% cotton, 30% Merino wool
(approx 218yd/200m per 100g)
2[3:3] x 100g skeins in 25 Turquoise
5.5mm needles
5.5mm circular or double-pointed
    needles
Stitch markers

Note: Yarn amounts given are based on average requirements and are approximate.

TENSION

17 sts and 25 rows to 4in (10cm) over st st.
17 sts and 25 rows to 4in (10cm) over lace patt.
Each lace patt rep meas 4in wide x 1½in long (10 x 4cm).
Use smaller or larger needles if necessary to obtain correct tension.

PATTERN NOTES

This shrug starts with the centre back lace panel. Stitches are then picked up on one side, knitted back and forth and then joined in the round to form the sleeve. The second side is worked in the same way. Sleeves can be made shorter or longer – this style would work really well with a three-quarter sleeve to show off some funky bangles. Our model is size 6-8 and wears size 2.

HEART VINE LACE PATTERN

Worked over 17 sts and 10 rows

Row 1 (RS): K2, p2, k1, yo, k1, k2tog, p1, ssk, k1, yo, k1, p2, k2.

Row 2 and all WS rows: P2, k2, p4, k1, p4, k2, p2.

Row 3: As row 1.

Row 5: K2, p2, k2, k2tog, yo, p1, yo, ssk, k2, p2, k2.

Row 7: K2, p2, k1, k2tog, yo, k1, p1, k1, yo, ssk, k1, p2, k2.

Row 9: K2, p2, k2tog, yo, k2, p1, k2, yo, ssk, p2, k2.

Row 10: P2, k2, p4, k1, p4, k2, p2.

These 10 rows form pattern and are repeated.

SHRUG

CENTRAL LACE PANEL

Cast on 17 sts.

Knit 2 rows.

Next row (WS): K1, (yo, k2tog) to end.

Knit 2 rows.

SET LACE PATT

Work Heart Vine Lace Patt over all sts, working 10-row patt 8[9:10] times in total.

Piece meas approx 13¼[15:16½]in (34[38:42]cm).

Knit 2 rows.

HEART VINE LACE PATTERN

KEY

	RS: knit, WS: purl
•	RS: purl, WS: knit
O	yo
/	k2tog
\	ssk

Next row (RS): K1, (yo, k2tog) to end.
Knit 2 rows.
Cast off loosely.

SIDE SECTION (MAKE 2)

With RS facing, pick up and k4 sts along
first border, 64[72:80] sts along lace
panel and 4 sts along second border.
72[80:88] sts.
Next row (WS): K4, p to last 4 sts, k4.
Next row: Knit.
Next row: K1, ssk, yo, k1, p to last 4 sts,
k1, yo, k2tog, k1.
Next row: Knit.
Next row: K4, p to last 4 sts, k4.

SET SIDE SHAPING

Row 1 (RS): K4, ssk, k to last 6 sts,
k2tog, k4. 70[78:86] sts.
Row 2: K1, ssk, yo, k1, p to last 4 sts, k1,
yo, k2tog, k1.
Row 3: Knit.
Row 4: K4, p to last 4 sts, k4.
Rep these 4 rows 7[11:15] more times
(56 sts).
Keeping lace border patt correct,
cont straight until piece meas approx
9½[11:12½]in (24[28:32]cm), ending
with row 4 and working kfb into last st.

SHAPE SLEEVE

Join in the round, working first st
(increased on last rnd) tog with last st
of previous rnd to form a neat join. Pm
to denote beg of rnd.
Rib rnd: (K1, p1) around, slipping marker.
Work 19 more rnds in rib.
Next rnd (dec): Rib to last st, remove
marker, sk2po, pm (54 sts).
Rib 2 rnds.
Rep last 3 rnds 8 more times (38 sts).
Rib 24 rnds straight.
Cast off loosely.

TO FINISH

Weave in ends.
Block to open out lace pattern.

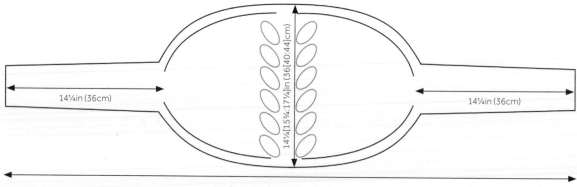

14¼in (36cm)

14¼[15¾:17¼]in (36[40:44]cm)

14¼in (36cm)

51¼[54¼:57½]in (103[138:146]cm)

Techniques

All the skills you need
to get knitting.

CASTING ON

The knitted cast on is useful because it uses many of the same moves as the knit stitch, so you can practise before you even start. The long-tail method creates a stretchier edge.

KNITTED CAST ON

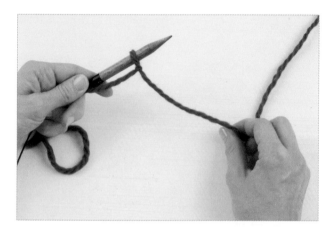

1 Start with a slipknot. Slip it on to your left-hand needle and tighten it to fit, but not so that it doesn't move easily along the needle.

2 Keeping your slipknot on the left-hand needle, insert your right-hand needle into the loop, from left to right, underneath the left-hand needle. (If it is tricky to do this, your slipknot is too tight – tug on the loop to loosen it.)

3 Bring the working yarn clockwise underneath the right-hand needle and back over the top, so you make a loop around it closer to the needle tips than the original slipknot. Use the tip of the right-hand needle to pull this new loop through the original slipknot.

4 Bring this new loop around to the tip of the left-hand needle and slip it on. You now have two stitches on the left-hand needle. To cast on more stitches, insert your right-hand needle into this new stitch and repeat steps 2–4. Repeat as many times as your pattern calls for.

LONG-TAIL CAST ON

1 To start a long-tail cast on, make a slipknot in your yarn, leaving a long tail of around 1in (2.5cm) for each stitch to be cast on, and slip it on to your needle.

2 With your left hand, create a slingshot shape by pointing your index finger and wrapping the working yarn clockwise over it, then raising your thumb and wrapping the tail anticlockwise over that. Curl the remaining three fingers in to grasp the yarn ends.

3 Use the needle tip to pick up the strand of yarn around the outside of your thumb, forming a loop.

4 Then pick up the strand of yarn on the inside of your index finger and pull it through the loop.

5 Let the yarn go and pull to tighten, but not too tight. You now have two stitches cast on. Repeat steps 2–5 until you have cast on the required number of stitches.

KNIT STITCH

The knit stitch is the basic building block of knitting. If you can work a knit stitch, you can knit: it's that simple.

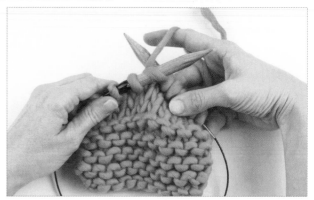

1 Hold the needle with the stitches on in your left hand and insert the tip of the right-hand needle into the first stitch, underneath the left-hand needle. The needle goes through the stitch from left to right.

2 Take the working yarn underneath and back over the right-hand needle in a clockwise direction, creating a loop in front of the stitch that is holding both needles.

3 Now use the tip of the right-hand needle to pull this loop through the original stitch.

4 The loop on your right-hand needle is the new stitch. Slip the original stitch off the end of the left-hand needle and let it fall. It now forms part of the fabric you are knitting.

5 Repeat steps 1–4 with the next stitch on the left-hand needle and then the following one until you have knitted every stitch. To knit the next row, simply turn the work around, take the right-hand needle – now with all the stitches on – in your left hand and start all over again.

PURL STITCH

The purl stitch is the mirror image of the knit stitch. All knitting patterns, no matter how complicated, are created from knit and purl stitches.

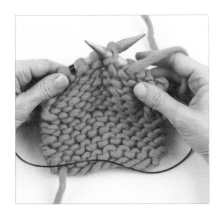

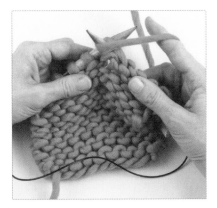

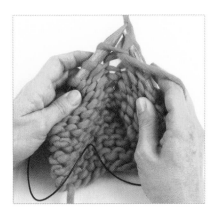

1 Insert the tip of your right-hand needle into the front of the first stitch on the left-hand needle from right to left, with the right-hand needle in front of the left-hand needle.

2 Take the working yarn clockwise underneath the right-hand needle tip and back over it, creating a new loop in front of the stitch being worked.

3 Pull the right-hand needle tip back out of the stitch, taking the new loop of yarn with it. This is now the new stitch.

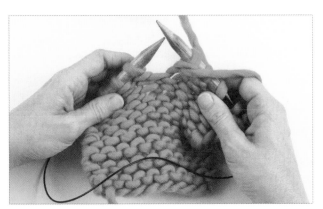

4 Let the original stitch slip off the left-hand needle to form part of the fabric.

5 Repeat steps 1–4 in the next stitch on the left-hand needle, and then the next, until all stitches have been purled. The fabric will look bobbly on the purled side and smoother on the knitted side. If you knit all the right-side rows and purl all the wrong-side rows, it is called stocking stitch – this is the most common stitch pattern you will see.

KNITTING IN THE ROUND

There are a few ways to knit in the round: you can use several double-pointed needles or a circular needle exactly the right size for your knit. The magic loop method is handy because you can use the same circular needle for any size of knitting.

1 Cast on the number of stitches you want and slide them on to the connecting cable of your circular needle.

2 Find the middle of the stitches and pull the cable out through this point, but not so far that any stitches drop off the ends of the needle tips.

3 Leave the half of the stitches connected to the working yarn on the cable – these will be known as the back stitches. Slide the other half of the stitches on to the left-hand needle tip. These are the front stitches.

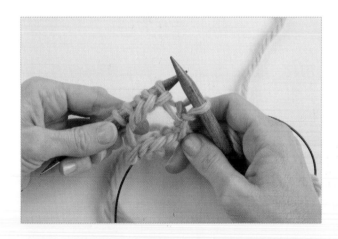

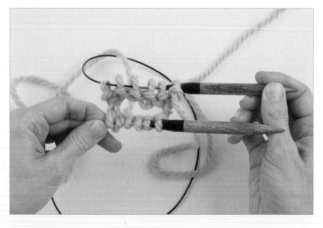

4 Bring the right-hand needle tip around and knit the first stitch on the left-hand needle tip. Pull the working yarn tightly afterwards; you will find your stitches have joined in a loop. It is a good idea to place a marker at this point so that you know where your round begins and ends.

5 Carry on knitting until you have worked all the front stitches. Taking care not to flip the stitches you have worked upside down or inside out, turn the work so the stitches you have just knitted sit at the back on the left-hand needle tip and the cast-on stitches are at the front on the cable.

JOGLESS JOIN

Sometimes, joining in the round can leave a gap or irregularity that needs to be patched up at the end of the project. This simple trick is a way to avoid that and create a really neat join.

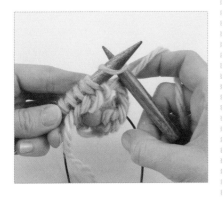

6 Pull the cable until the cast-on stitches now at the front of the work are sitting on the needle tip in front of the other needle tip. This is now your left-hand needle. Take care not to drop any stitches at this point. Pull the needle tip at the back out of the back stitches so that they sit on the cable. This is now your right-hand needle tip. Bring this needle tip around and work the first stitch on the left-hand needle. Carry on knitting until you have worked all the stitches on the needle tip. You have now knitted one round. Repeat for as many rounds as you like, creating a neat tube of knitting.

1 Cast on one more stitch than you need. Once the stitches have been distributed across your needles, slip the last cast-on stitch on to the first needle.

2 Use your fingers or a needle tip to pass the first cast-on stitch over the last cast-on stitch.

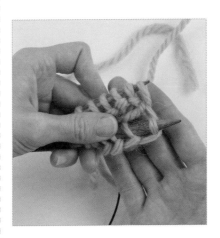

3 Now return the last cast-on stitch to its original needle. The result is a really neat, tight join.

TOP TIP
When knitting in the round, avoid ladders of loose stitches by making sure you move the gap between needles regularly. A simple way to do this is to slide the cable out so that all the stitches line up, then pull it out at a different point to continue your magic loop.

INCREASING

Increasing stitches makes your fabric wider. 'Make one left' (m1L) creates a left-slanted increase, whereas 'make one right' (m1R) creates a right-slanted increase. 'Knit front and back' (kfb) turns one stitch into two. Working increases and decreases one stitch in from the edge gives you a smooth, neat edge to your work.

MAKE ONE LEFT (MIL)

1 Knit the first stitch on the needle, then find the bar that sits between this stitch and the next on the left-hand needle. Insert the tip of the right-hand needle from front to back through this bar, pick it up and slip it on to the tip of the left-hand needle.

2 Knit this new stitch through the back loop (see facing page). This twists it and avoids a hole.

MAKE ONE RIGHT (MIR)

1 Pick up the bar before the next stitch on the right-hand needle. Insert the tip of the right-hand needle from back to front into this bar, pick it up and slip it on to the tip of the left-hand needle.

2 Knit this stitch through the front loop. This twists it and avoids a hole.

KNIT FRONT AND BACK (KFB)

1 Before you begin, take a look at the first stitch on your left-hand needle. The front of the loop (on the side of the needle facing you) should be a little in front of the back of the loop. These are also known as the front and back legs of the stitch. Start off by knitting the first stitch through its front loop as normal, but do not slip the stitch off the end of the left-hand needle.

2 Keeping the original stitch on the left-hand needle and the new stitch on the right-hand needle, take the right-hand needle tip to the back of the left-hand needle and insert it into the back loop of the original stitch.

3 Wrap the yarn around and pull the new loop through as you would in the knit stitch, then slip the original stitch off the end of the left-hand needle. You now have two stitches on the right-hand needle knitted from just one stitch on the left-hand needle.

K TBL

Knitting through the back loop can close a gap or twist a stitch to make it stand out.

Most of the time when you knit you insert the tip of the right-hand needle into the front loop of the stitch you are knitting. Inserting the needle tip into the back of the stitch, as shown here, is called 'knitting through the back loop' and twists the stitch, which can give it extra definition. Sometimes this technique is used to untwist stitches that have ended up twisted for one reason or another.

YARN OVERS

Yarn overs form the basis of all lace knitting. They can be used to create decorative eyelets or as an alternative way of increasing. They work slightly differently depending on the stitch that follows and they sometimes have different names but in this book they are all called yarn overs.

YARN OVER BEFORE A KNIT STITCH

Also known as yarn forward (yf or yfwd), yarn over needle (yon).

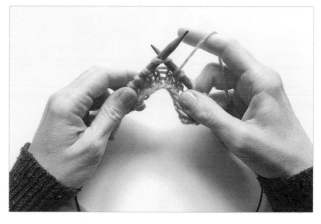

1 After your last stitch bring the yarn to the front of the work...

2 ...then knit the next stitch as normal, taking the working yarn over the top of the needle to the back of the work.

3 The working yarn has created a new stitch, which you can work as if it were a normal stitch on the next row.

4 This leaves a little hole in the fabric. It works in exactly the same way if you are working a knit decrease in your next stitch, even if you are slipping a stitch before you work your knit decrease. To avoid a hole, you can work the yarn over through the back loop on the next row.

YARN OVER BEFORE A PURL STITCH

Also known as yarn round needle (yrn), yarn over and round needle (yorn).

1 After your last stitch bring the yarn to the front of the needle if it isn't there already.

2 Take it over the needle to the back of the work, then bring it between the needles to the front of the work.

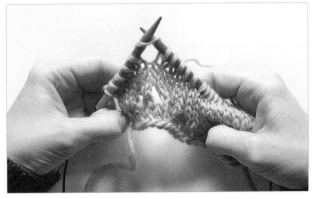

3 Purl the next stitch as normal.

4 On the next row, work the yarn over as if it were a normal stitch to create an eyelet, or work it through the back loop to avoid a hole. The yarn over works in the same way if you are working a purl decrease on the following stitch.

DECREASING

'Knit two together' (k2tog) is the simplest decrease and creates a right-leaning stitch. You can purl two together in a similar way. 'Slip, slip, knit' (ssk) makes a left-leaning decrease. 'Slip one, knit two together, pass slipped stitch over' (sk2po) makes a double decrease.

KNIT TWO TOGETHER (K2TOG)

1 Instead of inserting your needle into just one stitch, insert it into the next two stitches on the left-hand needle, just as if you were going to knit a single stitch. Wrap the working yarn around the needle and pull the new loop through the original two stitches.

2 Slip them off the end of the left-hand needle, just as you would if you were knitting a single stitch. You have now made two stitches into one stitch.

SLIP, SLIP, KNIT (SSK)

1 Insert the tip of the right-hand needle into the next stitch on the left-hand needle as if to knit it, but instead just slip it from the left-hand needle to the right-hand needle. Repeat with the next stitch so you have two slipped stitches on the right-hand needle.

2 Insert the left-hand needle through both those stitches from left to right in front of the right-hand needle. Wrap the working yarn around the right-hand needle, knitting the two slipped stitches together through the back loop, and slip them off the end of the left-hand needle.

SLIP ONE, KNIT TWO TOGETHER, PASS SLIPPED STITCH OVER (SK2PO)

1 Slip the next stitch from the left to the right-hand needle as if to knit.

2 Knit the following two stitches together.

3 Pass the slipped stitch over.

CABLES

Cables use an extra needle with two pointed ends called a cable needle to move stitches from one place to another. There are two basic types – with the cable needle held at the back or the front of the work – but endless variations.

CABLE FOUR FRONT (C4F)

1 Slip the next two stitches to a cable needle held at the front of the work.

2 Leaving these two stitches, knit the following two stitches as normal.

3 Now knit the two stitches on the cable needle.

4 You have created a left-leaning cable.

CABLE FOUR BACK (C4B)

1 Slip the next two stitches to a cable needle held at the back of the work.

2 Leaving these two stitches, knit the following two stitches as normal.

3 Now knit the two stitches on the cable needle.

4 You have created a right-leaning cable.

JUDY'S MAGIC CAST ON

'Judy's magic cast on' was invented by Judy Becker, who introduced it on knitty.com. It is a great way to start toe-up socks and other projects with an invisible, seamless base.

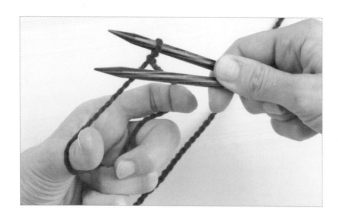

1 Hold two dpns (or the two tips of a circular needle if you're working with the magic loop method – see page 116) side by side. Leaving a long tail, make a slipknot and put it on the needle farther from you. This counts as your first stitch. Wrap the tail around your index finger and the working yarn around your thumb, as shown, and hold both ends in your remaining fingers.

2 Take the needle closer to you towards the yarn held by your index finger and wrap it around. It doesn't matter which way it wraps around the needle.

3 Now take the needle farther from you towards the yarn held by your thumb and wrap around. Again, it doesn't matter which way the yarn goes around the needle.

4 Repeat steps 2 and 3 until you have cast on the required number of stitches. On one side of the two rows of cast-on stitches there will be a little ridge. Make sure this ridge is facing up when you start knitting, so that it ends up on the inside of the sock.

5 To start knitting, hold the yarn tail tightly along the ridge of stitches. Before you work each stitch on this first round, check to see which leg is in front. If the rear leg of the stitch is in front of the front leg, knit the stitch through the back of the loop (see page 119). When the front leg of the stitch is in front, knit the stitch as normal.

SHADOW-WRAP SHORT ROWS

There are a number of ways to work the 'wrap and turn' used to avoid holes when shaping fabric using short rows. My favourite is the shadow-wrap method, invented by *Socktopus* author Alice Yu; this is very neat and less fiddly than some other methods.

1 Work up to the point where you are asked to wrap and turn in your pattern, then knit the stitch to be wrapped. Underneath this stitch you will notice the stitch that came before it – Alice calls this the 'mama' stitch, while the stitch on the needle is the 'daughter' stitch.

2 Lift the mama stitch on to the left-hand needle, taking care not to twist it, then knit it and drop it off. You now have two stitches on the right-hand needle, both coming out of the same mama stitch – the daughter stitch and the 'shadow' stitch.

3 Slip the stitch pair to the left-hand needle and turn to work the wrong side. Next time you come to these two stitches, you will work them together as if they were one stitch.

 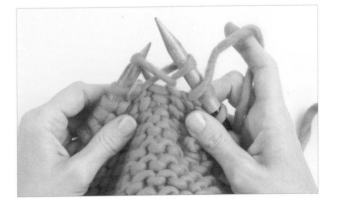

4 To work a shadow wrap purlwise, work to the stitch to be wrapped, then slip it purlwise on to the right-hand needle.

5 Lift the mama stitch of the slipped stitch on to the left-hand needle, being careful not to twist it, then purl it and drop the mama stitch off the needle. Once again, you have a daughter stitch and a shadow stitch coming out of the same mama stitch. Turn and work the right side. When you come to these stitches again, work them as if they were one stitch.

AFTERTHOUGHT HEEL

This simple technique lets you work a straight tube, then add on a heel, thumbhole or even buttonhole at the end

1 When you come to the point where your heel is to be worked, the pattern will tell you to work a section in contrasting scrap yarn, then work the same stitches again in your main yarn. Here the sock has been cast off and you can see the scrap yarn marking the point where the heel will be.

2 Use your needle tip to pick up stitches along one side of the scrap yarn. Make sure you only pick up one leg of the stitch at a time so the needle goes right through the stitch. If you pick up the right leg of each stitch you will end up with all your stitches facing in the right direction.

3 Here is the sock with one set of stitches picked up on a double-pointed needle.

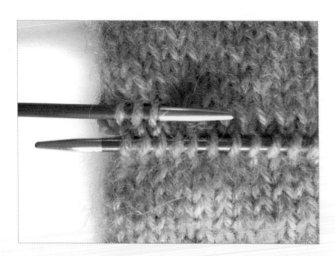

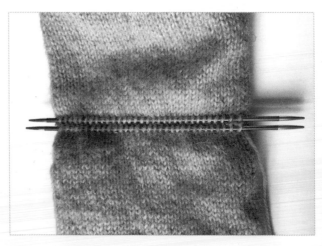

4 Once you have picked up all the stitches along one side, repeat the process on the other side of the scrap yarn.

5 Here you can see all the stitches sitting on two double-pointed needles.

6 Now carefully remove the scrap yarn from the stitches you have picked up.

7 This image shows the gap you have created, with all the stitches held safely on dpns.

8 Now pick up one or two stitches in the gaps between the two needles, according to your pattern.

9 Start knitting the stitches according to your pattern – in this case you can see I'm working in a contrast yarn.

10 This is the finished afterthought heel.

ONE-COLOUR BRIOCHE

Brioche knitting is widely reputed to be challenging, but in fact it is one of the simplest and most pleasing techniques I've encountered. Using slipped stitches and yarn overs worked together on the next row, it creates a squashy, reversible ribbed fabric and a wonderful colour effect when worked in two shades. Brioche also has a lovely rhythm that is perfect for knitters who want their craft to be about relaxation and wellbeing.

1 Brioche starts with a set-up row. The order of knitted and slipped stitches will vary from pattern to pattern; in this case, we will start with a simple knit stitch. *Bring the yarn to the front of the work.

2 Slip the next stitch purlwise, still holding the yarn at the front of the work.

3 Knit the next stitch as normal, creating a yarn over across the slipped stitch. Repeat from * to the end of the row, or as your pattern directs.

4 On the next row, you will see ordinary knit stitches alternating with slipped stitches with a yarn over. As you come to each knit stitch, bring the yarn to the front, then slip the stitch purlwise, as in step 2. This is known as slip one, yarn over (sl1yo).

5 The next stitch is a slipped stitch with a yarn over across it. Knit the slipped stitch together with its yarn over. This is called brioche knit 1, or brk1. It will also create a yarn over across the stitch you just slipped.

6 Continue to work in this way until you are directed otherwise by your pattern. Each row is worked in the same way, regardless of whether it is a RS or a WS row. The result is a reversible ribbed fabric.

TWO-COLOUR BRIOCHE IN THE ROUND

If you've never tried brioche before, this is a great way to start. It introduces you to all the basics of brioche knitting, but is actually simpler than two-colour brioche knitted flat. Once you've got the hang of it in the round, you'll have no trouble with the flat version.

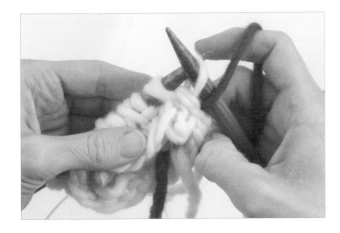

1 Cast on with A and join in the round, then work a set-up round of (sl1yo, k1). The next round is worked in B. Leaving A hanging at the back of the work, join B at the back of the work but bring it to the front to work the first stitch, which is a sl1yo.

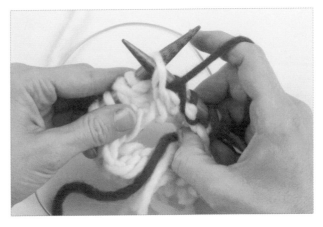

2 Using B work brp1, purling the stitch together with its yarn over. Continue to work (sl1yo, brp1) around.

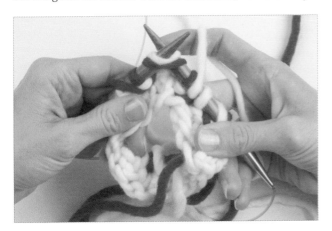

3 The next round is worked in A. Work (sl1yo, brk1) around. These two rounds are repeated. The result is a lovely two-colour rib effect, with A dominant on one side and B on the other.

BRIOCHE INCREASES

Because brioche stitches work with ribs in pairs of two stitches, increasing and decreasing is a little more challenging than with plain knitting.

TWO-STITCH INCREASE (BRKYOBRK)

1 Brioche knit the next stitch and its yarn over, but don't slip the stitches off the needle.

2 Bring the yarn forward...

3 ... then brioche knit 1 again into the same stitches, creating a yarn over between the 2 brk stitches.

4 Slip the original stitches off the LH needle – you have increased two stitches, or one set of brioche ribs.

TOP TIP
Brioche increases in themselves are pretty straightforward – it's on the next row that things can get confusing, when you are changing from working brioche stitches to simple stitches. Make sure you keep track of all your stitches: if you're having trouble it may be worth placing a marker at the increased stitch so you know when you come to it on the next row.

FOUR-STITCH INCREASE (BR4STINC)

1 Brioche knit the next stitch and its yarn over but don't slip the stitch off the needle.

2 Bring the yarn forward...

3 ...brioche knit the same stitch and yarn over again...

4 ...bring the yarn forward again...

5 ...and brioche knit the same stitch and its yarn over one more time.

6 Now slip the original stitch and yarn over off the needle. You have increased four stitches, or two brioche ribs.

SHORT ROWS IN TWO-COLOUR BRIOCHE

This is a rather fiddly little technique that will give you a flattering scooped hem at the back of your sweater while keeping your two-colour brioche ribs nice and neat.

1 Using A, work to 2 sts past the halfway point marker, ending with sl1yo.

2 Change to a spare 5.5mm circular needle (I have used a striped metal needle) and patt to last 4 sts, again ending with sl1yo.

3 Take yarn to front and slip next st and its yo to right-hand needle – the spare one.

4 Take yarn to back, then slip 3 rem sts of rnd to right-hand needle.

5 Using B and main 5.5mm needle, (sl1yo, brp1) from start of rnd to start of spare needle, then work across spare needle to wrapped st.

6 Take yarn to front and slip wrapped st to right-hand (main) needle, then take yarn to back so the stitch is wrapped twice – once each with A and B. Slip rem 3 sts of rnd from spare needle back to other end of main needle.

7 Turn work so wrong side is facing and, with both working yarns in front, slip wrapped st to main needle.

8 Using spare needle and A, (sl1yo, brp1) to 5 sts before halfway point marker.

9 Sl1yo, then with yarn in front, slip next st and its yo to right-hand (spare) needle.

10 Take yarn to back. Slide sts on spare needle to the other end to work wrong side again.

11 Using B and spare needle, (brk1, sl1yo) to st before wrapped st, brk1. Main needle now holds all sts not in the short row.

12 Take B to front and slip wrapped stitch. Take yarn to back and turn, then slip wrapped st to main needle.

13 Using A and spare needle, (sl1yo, brk1) to last 5 sts on spare needle, sl1yo, take yarn to front and slip stitch.

14 Take yarn to back and slip 3 unworked sts to main needle as foll: first to right-hand (spare) needle, then back to main needle.

15 Slide sts to other end of spare needle and, using B, (brp1, sl1yo) to last st before wrapped st, brp1, yf and slip st, yb. Turn and slip wrapped st to main needle.

16 Rep from step 8, ending with a WS short row in B. Turn work. With both yarns in front and RS facing, slip last wrapped st from spare to main needle.

17 Using spare needle and A, patt to end of spare needle, then to end of rnd, working first wrapped st as foll: slip to right-hand needle then use left-hand needle tip to pick up double wrap.

18 Slip both on to left-hand needle and brk together. Work all wrapped sts tog in the same way.

19 Once you have reached end of the rnd, slide sts on spare needle to other end and use main needle tip and B to work across them again.

20 All sts are now back on main needle. Using A, return to working in the round, working all wrapped stitches together with wraps as in steps 17 and 18.

JAPANESE SHORT ROWS

Japanese short rows are simple to work and barely visible, making them perfect for bust darts. You will need several lockable stitch markers, one for each turn you will make.

1 Knit to the point where you want to turn, turn the work and place a lockable stitch marker on the working yarn. This picture shows the WS of the work after turning.

2 Slip the next stitch purlwise.

3 Then continue purling. This image shows the stitch marker held in place between two stitches.

4 Purl to the next point where you want to turn.

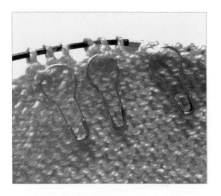

5 Place a lockable stitch marker on the working yarn and turn the work so the RS is facing.

6 Knit to the next place your pattern tells you to turn and repeat from step 2. This image shows the work after you have turned it, before placing the lockable stitch marker on the working yarn.

7 Continue working in this way. Once you have worked several short rows, you will have several lockable stitch markers sitting at the back of your work.

8 Now it's time to start working back across the short rows. Work to the first point where you want to close up a short row gap. You can see the stitch marker sitting at the back of the work here.

9 Pull on the stitch marker to make a loop, then slip this loop on to the LH needle. Remove the stitch marker.

10 Knit this loop together with the next stitch on the needle to close up the gap.

11 Turn the work and repeat steps 2 and 3, then work to the next stitch marker and repeat steps 9-11.

12 On your next turn you will repeat steps 9 and 10, then carry on working on the same side to the next stitch marker along and repeat steps 9-11.

13 Continue working in this way until you have closed all the original gaps, then return to working in the round. One stitch marker will remain in place on your first round – when you come to this, use it to pull up a loop, place it on the LH needle and work it together with the next stitch.

14 This image shows a neatly defined bust dart with barely visible short row turns.

SEAMLESS POCKETS

I love working pockets and linings without sewing – it's a little bit involved but a lot of fun!

1 At the point where you are going to work your pocket or lining, your pattern will direct you to make a series of yarn over increases. Here you can see where a number of yarn overs have been made in between stitches.

2 On the next row or round, work to the point where the yarn overs are and slip the first yarn over on to a spare needle.

3 Then work the next stitch according to your pattern using your main needle. Make sure the working yarn is between the two needles for purl stitches and behind the main needle for knit stitches, so it doesn't get caught up in the yarn overs. Here it is in between after working a purl stitch.

4 At the end of the row or round you are back to the original stitch count on your main needle and all the increased stitches are sitting on the spare needle.

5 Now put your main stitches on hold and work the lining as directed by your pattern – here I'm working in stocking stitch in a contrast yarn. Slip the stitch at the beginning of each row to make it easy to join the stitches later on. When your lining is as long as you want it to be, put these stitches on hold and return to your main piece.

6 When you come to the lining section, work the first main stitch together with the first, slipped, lining stitch. Then work the main stitches that sit across the lining stitches in your pattern and work the last, slipped, lining stitch together with the corresponding stitch of the main piece. You will only work these joining rows on every alternate row.

7 Once you have worked the main piece to match the lining you will finish this section off. In the case of the *Lilies of the Field* camisole this means joining the two sections in a three-needle cast off, shown here in the contrast yarn.

8 To finish a pocket, work to the start of the lined section, slip the pocket stitches of the main piece on hold and work across the lining section as detailed in your pattern.

9 Once you have cast off, you can work the pocket tops. Slip the held stitches back on to your needles. Traditional patterns will simply work these stitches then sew the pocket tops down at the end, but to avoid this, at the start of each right-side row pick up a stitch from the main body of the piece and work it together with the first lining stitch, then do the same at the end of the pocket top.

10 Here you can see all the stitches for the pocket top in a contrast yarn. Continue working as in step 9, picking up a stitch from the main body at each end of every right-side row, until you have finished working the pocket top.

11 Finally cast off, leaving your pocket complete.

STRANDED COLOURWORK

Some patterns call for you to work more than one colour in the same row. In this book we strand the colour not in use behind the colour being worked in a technique sometimes known as Fairisle, after Fair Isle in Shetland, Scotland, which is famous for colourful knits using this technique.

HOLDING YARN FOR COLOURWORK KNITTING
There are two ways to hold multiple yarns when working colourwork:

- Two-handed: hold one yarn in the 'English' style in your right hand and the other in the 'continental' style in your left.

- One-handed: wind the different yarns around the same hand and pick the one you want when it comes to each stitch. You can buy knitting 'thimbles' that help keep yarns organized when working in this way.

WORKING STRANDED COLOURWORK
Most colourwork patterns are set out in a chart. Each different-coloured square represents a different stitch.

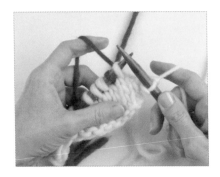

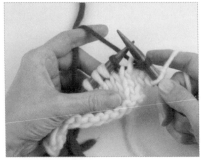

1 Work the required number of stitches in the first colour.

2 Then work the required number of stitches in the second colour.

3 The yarn not in use is stranded at the back of the fabric. To avoid long strands that may get caught on things or pull on the fabric if they end up being too tight, you need to catch the yarn not in use at regular intervals. I would recommend doing this every two or three stitches. This also helps to keep your tension even. To catch the yarn not in use, simply lift it up and take the working yarn across it as you work the next stitch.

4 This will secure it at the back of the fabric...

5 ...but won't show through at the front.

INTARSIA IN THE ROUND

Traditionally intarsia is worked back and forth, and in a sense that is still the case when you're working in the round as you work both sides of the fabric.

1 At the start of the first round of your intarsia motif, make a yarn over, then work to the point where your motif starts.

2 Join a new colour, twisting the yarns together by bringing the new colour up from left to right underneath the old colour. This image shows a round several rows into the motif, where you can clearly see the colour change. At the end of the motif join a new ball or bobbin of the colour and continue to the last stitch of the round.

3 Knit the last stitch of the round together with the yarn over at the start of the round using ssk.

4 Turn the work so the wrong side is facing and start the round with a yarn over, then purl to the motif.

5 Twist the yarns together as before to avoid holes and purl across the motif, then purl to the last stitch.

6 Purl together the last stitch of the round with the yarn over at the beginning of the round.

7 Repeat steps 1-6 until the motif is complete, then continue working in the round with the right side facing. The result is a neat join at the start of the round.

HOLDING YARN DOUBLE

Working with two strands of yarn held together is a great way of blending colours to create a marled effect, mixing different fibres to add textural interest or simply doubling up a yarn to make it thicker and quicker to knit.

1 Hold the two yarns together as if you were holding only one strand of yarn. Check your yarn balls from time to time to make sure they're not getting tangled.

2 When you come to a stitch made from two strands of yarn, just knit them both together as if it were a single stitch made from just one strand.

PICKING UP STITCHES

Picking up stitches from the edge of knitting is great for adding on neat finishing bands and a way to avoid sewing.

1 With the right side of the fabric facing you and starting in the bottom right-hand corner, *insert the tip of your right-hand needle into the fabric.

2 Pull a loop of working yarn through this hole to create a stitch on your right-hand needle.

3 Repeat from * as directed by your pattern. You can now work these picked-up stitches just like normal stitches.

HALF TREBLE CROCHET BOBBLE

This pretty little bobble is quick and easy to work

1 Work to the point where your pattern tells you to make the bobble, then using a crochet hook, pull a loop up from your next stitch.

2 Put the yarn over the hook...

3 ... then pull up a loop so you have three loops over your hook. You can drop the first stitch off the needle.

4 Repeat step 2 two more times so you have seven loops on your hook.

5 Yarn over hook and pull it through all seven loops, then chain one.

6 Bring the hook to the front and lift up the left leg of the stitch in the row below.

7 Yarn over hook and pull this through the two loops on the hook.

8 Slip this loop – and the completed bobble – on to the right-hand needle.

9 This is the finished bobble in situ.

CASTING OFF

Cast off your knits securely by lifting each live stitch over the next.

1 Start by working the first two stitches as normal: if it is a knit stitch, knit it; if it is a purl stitch, purl it unless your pattern says otherwise.

2 Use the tip of your left-hand needle to lift the first stitch on the right-hand needle up, over the top of the second stitch and off the end of the right-hand needle. This stitch is now cast off.

3 Knit the next stitch on the left-hand needle so that you again have two stitches on the right-hand needle, then repeat step 2.

4 Keep repeating step 3 until you have one stitch left on the right-hand needle and none on the left-hand needle. Pass the rest of the ball, or the end of the working yarn, through this last stitch, using your fingers to make the stitch big enough for the ball to fit through, then pull tightly on the working yarn. You should have a neat and tidy row of cast-off stitches.

THREE-NEEDLE CAST OFF

This is a great way to cast off, avoid sewing and create a seam, which can add useful structure to a knit.

1 Start with your two pieces each on a needle tip, with the right sides together.

2 Here the working yarn is still attached to one side, but if it's not simply join a new strand of yarn. You will need a third needle to work the cast off.

3 Hold the two needles with the two pieces on together in your left hand, then insert the third needle into the first stitch on both needles.

4 Knit these two stitches together.

5 Repeat steps 3 and 4 to knit a second stitch on to the right-hand needle.

6 Lift the first stitch over the second stitch to cast it off.

7 Repeat steps 3-6 until you have cast off all stitches, then fasten off the last stitch. Here the seam is on the wrong side.

8 And this image shows the neat join on the right side.

GRAFTING

Kitchener stitch allows you to graft two sets of live stitches together seamlessly, making it perfect for the toes of socks and jumper underarms.

1 This image shows two sets of live stitches at the end of an afterthought heel, held one behind the other on double-pointed needles. The stitch marker shows the beginning of the round.

2 Break the working yarn leaving a long tail and thread the end on to a large-eyed darning or tapestry needle. I have used a contrast yarn to show the steps more clearly. Insert the tapestry needle into the first stitch on the front knitting needle as if to purl, pull it through but do not drop the stitch off the needle.

3 Insert the tapestry needle into the first stitch on the back needle as if to knit, pull it through but do not drop the stitch off.

4 Now insert the tapestry needle into the first stitch on the front needle as if to knit.

5 Pull it through and drop the stitch off the needle.

6 Insert the tapestry needle into the new first stitch on the front needle as if to purl, pull it through but do not drop the stitch off the needle.

7 Insert the tapestry needle into the first stitch on the back needle as if to purl.

8 Pull it through and drop the stitch off the needle.

9 Now insert the tapestry needle into the new first stitch on the back needle as if to knit. Pull it through but do not drop it off the needle.

10 Repeat steps 4–9 until two stitches remain on the needles, then repeat steps 4, 5, 7 and 8 again. All the stitches have now been grafted using the tapestry needle. Now use the tip of the tapestry needle to tighten up any loose stitches.

11 Here you can see a neat row of contrast stitches that joins the two sections.

12 Worked in the same yarn as the knitting, the join is invisible.

WEAVING IN ENDS

Tidy up loose ends by weaving them into the knitting following the knitted yarn. This technique is called Swiss darning or duplicate stitch, and can also be used to embroider.

1 When you come to the end of a project, you'll have a number of ends waiting to be woven in on the wrong side of the work. Choose a large-eyed tapestry needle – blunt or sharp tips should work equally well. With the wrong side facing (in the case of a stocking-stitch project, that's the purl side), thread a yarn end through the eye of the needle. The back of the work is made up of a series of curved stitches: I will call them bowls (which dip downwards) and hats (which curve upwards). Starting with the stitch next to your loose end, insert your needle first underneath the hat next to it, then, following the stitch already running through those loops, upwards through the bowl above it on the right-hand side. Miss out the next hat, upwards and to the left of your working yarn.

2 Insert the needle downwards and to the right into the next bowl to the left of your working yarn, and then through the hat beneath and to the right of it.

3 Miss out the next bowl, then insert your needle upwards and to the right, as in step 1.

4 Repeat steps 1–3 until you have a row of stitches duplicating the stitches in the knitting and neatly securing the loose end. Keep checking your stitches aren't showing on the right side of the work.

5 Your weaving should be completely invisible on the right side, and the fabric remains nice and stretchy.

FIXING MISTAKES

When I was making *Force field* I missed one of the buttonholes.
The technique I used to repair this can be used to mend all sorts of mistakes.

1 Here I've marked the point I want to unravel down to by inserting a small cable needle into the two stitches I want to get to.

2 I've knitted to the two stitches above where the buttonhole should be and dropped them off the needle.

3 In this image you can see how they've unravelled. The cable needle I inserted at the start has stopped them from going too far.

4 I've now knitted the two stitches held on the cable needle using scrap yarn in a contrast colour.

5 Now I'm using a crochet hook to re-knit the stitches up to the row of live stitches I started on. While one of the stitches remains on the cable needle, I've inserted the crochet hook from front to back through the other stitch and pulled through the first bar above the stitch – you can see all the bars like a ladder in image 3.

6 Taking care not to get the bars in the wrong order, I repeat step 5 until I come to the row of live stitches, then slip both of them back on to the left-hand needle and continue working as before.

7 Here you can see the two stitches in scrap yarn where the buttonhole should be. Once you have finished knitting, you can work these as you would an afterthought heel or thumb. These steps can help you fix all sorts of mistakes in knitting.

ABBREVIATIONS

k	knit
p	purl
alt	alternate
beg	begin/ning
brk1	brioche knit 1: k the next st and its yo tog
brp1	brioche purl 1: p the next st and its yo tog
br4stinc	brioche 4-st increase: (brk1, yo, brk1, yo, brk1) all into 1 st (increase 4)
C3Bp	cable 3 back pwise: slip next st to cn and hold at back, k2, p1 from cn
C3Fp	cable 3 front pwise: slip next 2 sts to cn and hold at front, p1, k2 from cn
C4B	cable 4 back: slip next 2 sts to cn and hold at back, k2, k2 from cn
C4F	cable 4 front: slip next 2 sts to cn and hold at front, k2, k2 from cn
C4Bp	cable 4 back pwise: slip next 2 sts to cn and hold at back, k2, p2 from cn
C4Fp	cable 4 front pwise: slip next 2 sts to cn and hold at front, p2, k2 from cn
C8Br	cable 8 back brioche: slip next 4 sts to cn and hold at back, (brk1, sl1yo) twice, (brk1, sl1yo) twice from cn
C8Brib	cable 8 back rib: slip next 4 sts to cn and hold at back, k1, p2, k1 from LH needle, k1, p2, k1 from cn
C8Frib	cable 8 front rib: slip next 4 sts to cn and hold at front, k1, p2, k1 from LH needle, k1, p2, k1 from cn
ch	chain
cl3	cluster 3 sts: insert RH needle tip into third st on LH needle and lift this over the first 2 sts and off the end of the needle, then work k1, yo, k1
cm	centimetre/s
cn	cable needle
cont	continue
Cr3L	cross 3 left: slip next 2 sts (k and p) to cn and hold at front, k1 tbl from LH needle, slip p st from cn back to LH needle and p it, k1 tbl from cn
Cr3R	cross 3 right: slip next 2 sts (k and p) to cn and hold at back, k1 tbl from LH needle, bring cn to front, slip p st from cn back to LH needle and p it, k1 tbl from cn
dc	double crochet
dec	decrease
dpn(s)	double-pointed needle(s)

foll	follows/following
g	gramme/s
g st	garter stitch: when knitting back and forth, knit every row; in the round work 1 rnd knit, 1 rnd purl
htr	half treble crochet
in	inch/es
inc	increase
k2tog	knit 2 stitches together (decrease 1)
k3tog	knit 3 stitches together (decrease 2)
kfb	knit into front and back of next stitch (increase 1)
kwise	knitwise
kyok	(k1, yo, k1) all into next st (increase 2)
kyokyok	(k1, yo, k1, yo, k1) all into next st (increase 4)
LH	left hand
RH	right hand
m	marker
m1	make 1 stitch: pick up the bar between 2 sts and knit it (increase 1)
m2	make 2 stitches: pick up the bar between 2 sts and k into the back and then front of it (increase 2)
m1L	pick up the bar between 2 sts from front to back, then knit it tbl (increase 1)
m1R	pick up the bar between 2 sts from back to front, then knit into front of it (increase 1)
m1p	make 1 purlwise (increase 1)
m1Lp	pick up the bar between 2 sts from front to back and p into the back of it (increase 1)
m1Rp	pick up the bar between 2 sts from back to front and p into it (increase 1)
MB	make htr crochet bobble (see page 141)
meas	measures
mm	millimetre/s
p2tog	purl 2 stitches together (decrease 1)
p3tog	purl 3 stitches together (decrease 2)
p2tog tbl	purl 2 together through the back loop: slip the next 2 sts one at a time to RH needle kwise, then slip them back to LH needle and ptog tbl
patt	pattern
PK1	pick up 1 slipped st from edge of Pocket Lining and k tog with next st
PP1	pick up 1 st from Body and p tog with next st
pm	place marker

psso	pass slipped stitch over
pwise	purlwise
rem	remain/ing
rep	repeat
rev st st	reverse stocking stitch: when knitting back and forth work RS purl, WS knit; in the round purl every rnd
rnd	round
RS/WS	right side/wrong side
skpo	slip 1, knit 1, pass the slipped stitch over (decrease 1)
sk2po	slip 1, knit 2 together, pass slipped stitch over (decrease 2)
s2kpo	slip 2 stitches one at a time kwise, knit 1, pass 2 slipped stitches over (decrease 2)
sp2po	slip one purlwise, purl 2 together, pass slipped stitch over (decrease 2)
sl st	slip stitch
sl1	slip 1 stitch
sl1p	slip 1 stitch purlwise
sl1yo	with yarn in front slip next st pwise, take yarn over needle to the back if the next st is a k or brk st; take yarn over needle to the back then in between the tips back to the front if the next st is a p or brp st. This creates a yarn over across the slipped stitch
sm	slip marker
ssk	slip next 2 stitches one at a time, kwise, to RH needle, insert tip of LH needle through both stitches and knit them together (decrease 1)

sssk	slip, slip, slip, knit: as ssk, but with 3 sts (decrease 2)
ssp	see p2tog tbl
sssp	as p2tog tbl, but with 3 sts (decrease 2)
st(s)	stitch(es)
st st	stocking stitch: when working back and forth, work RS knit, WS purl; in the round knit every rnd
tbl	through back loop
tog	together
tr	treble crochet
TW3	twisted 3-st cable: sl1 st to cn and hold at front, sl next st to another cn and hold at back, k1 tbl, then p1 from back cn, k1 tbl from front cn
w&t	wrap and turn
wyib	with yarn in the back
wyif	with yarn in the front
yb	yarn back
yf	yarn forward
yo	yarn over

Work each stitch as it appears: If the next st on the left-hand needle is 'flat' (ie purled on previous row) then knit this stitch, if the next stitch is a 'bump' (ie knitted on previous row) then purl this stitch.

CONVERSIONS

The patterns in this book use UK knitting terms. Below are the translations for US terms, which are sometimes different. We also include conversion tables for knitting needle sizes.

KNITTING NEEDLE SIZES

METRIC	UK	US	METRIC	UK	US
3.5mm	9	4	6mm	4	10
4mm	8	6	6.5mm	3	10½
4.5mm	7	7	8mm	0	1
5mm	6	8	10mm	000	15
5.5mm	5	9	12mm	–	17

KNITTING AND CROCHET TERMS

UK	US
cast off	bind off
moss stitch	seed stitch
stocking stitch	stockinette stitch
double crochet	single crochet
half treble crochet	half double crochet
treble crochet	double crochet

SUPPLIERS

BC GARN
SELECTED YARNS
selected-yarns.com

CAMAROSE
camarose.dk

CASCADE YARNS
cascadeyarns.com

GINGER'S HAND DYED
GINGER TWIST STUDIO
gingertwiststudio.com

JOHN ARBON TEXTILES
jarbon.com

KETTLE YARN CO
kettleyarnco.co.uk

LANG YARNS
langyarns.com

MCINTOSH
knitmcintosh.com

MANOS DEL URUGUAY
manos.uy

NEW LANARK SPINNING CO
newlanarkspinning.com

RAUWERK
rauwerk-wolle.de

RICO
rico-design.com

ROWAN
knitrowan.com

ACKNOWLEDGEMENTS

Thanks so much to the dream team who helped put this book together: designer extraordinaire Claire Stevens, pattern guru Rachel Vowles, amazing photographer Laurel Guilfoyle (laurel-guilfoyle.co.uk), hair and make-up magician Jen Dodson (jenidodson.com) and super helpful assistant and foot model, Maddie Tod. Most of the modelling in this book was done by the gorgeous Caitlin McCarthy (@curlycaitlin11), but big thanks to Lilla Varga, Lydia Jakeman, Caprice-Kwai Ambersley, Peter Harrap and Daisy Richardson who also feature (and to Maddie's feet).

I am indebted to a number of stitch dictionaries for inspiring or contributing to some of my patterns, including volumes by Hitomi Shida, Barbara G Walker and Wendy Bernard. I have also learnt much from designers I've written about, knitted patterns by and worked with over the years. I'd like to particularly thank Jo Allport and James McIntosh for listening ears, shoulders to cry on and general moral support, and to the lovely Erika Knight and Bella Harris who have really encouraged me as a designer.

Finally thanks so much to my family and friends, especially my wonderful husband Glen Richardson who steps in to do EVERYTHING when I'm in the throes of finishing a book, but still carries on making beautiful music and making me laugh every day. Thanks to my children Stan and Daisy, the sunshine of my life. Thanks to everyone who's taken the time to pour alcohol and coffee down my throat while listening to me complain or watching me frantically knit to meet a deadline, especially Liz and Juliet.

First published 2022 by
Guild of Master Craftsman Publications Ltd
Castle Place, 166 High Street, Lewes,
East Sussex BN7 1XU

ISBN 978 1 78494 634 0

A catalogue record for this book is available from the
British Library.

Publisher Jonathan Bailey
Production Manager Jim Bulley
Senior Project Editor Virginia Brehaut
Designer Claire Stevens
Illustrator Rachel Vowles
Assistant Maddie Tod

Colour origination by GMC Reprographics
Printed and bound in China

*Laburnum, Entwined, Golden shred, Shadow and light, Go
bananas, Magdalene* and *Pete's owls* previously published in
Knitting magazine. *Lux* is adapted from a design previously
published in *Knitting* magazine.

Picture Credits
Photographs by Laurel Guilfoyle, except for on the following
pages: 10: Jared Flood by Jared Flood, Erika Knight by
Georgina Piper, Elizabeth Zimmermann used with permission
from Schoolhouse Press; 112-146 techniques photography
by Anthony Bailey and Christine Boggis
Models Caitlin McCarthy (bameagency.com),
Lilla Varga (@lillabvarga), Lydia Jakeman (bameagency.com),
Caprice-Kwai Ambersley (zebedeetalent.com), Peter Harrap,
Daisy Richardson
Stitch charts designed using Stitchmastery
Hair and make-up Jen Dodson
Location Jassy's cosy secluded eco cabin near Brighton,
East Sussex, available as a holiday let via AirB&B. Additional
photography at Medley's Barn, Crowborough, East Sussex,
available as a holiday let via classic.co.uk

To order a book, contact:

GMC Publications Ltd,
Castle Place,
166 High Street,
Lewes, East Sussex,
BN7 1XU, United Kingdom
Tel: +44 (0)1273 488005
www.gmcbooks.com